A History of JEFFERSON

Marion County, Texas

THIRTEENTH PRINTING

JEFFERSON

Annual Historical Pilgrimage

GUARDING OAK

MUSEUM

One-Time Gateway of Texas
Retains Its Glory in Rush and Hurry
Of Modern Times

1836 - 1936

A HISTORY OF JEFFERSON

This pamphlet contains items of interest that we should know about our home town, and was compiled

by

Mrs. Arch McKay

Mrs. H. A. Spellings

Proceeds of sale to be used by Women's Auxiliary, Christ Episcopal Church.

THIRTEENTH PRINTING

These items have been taken from articles written

by various writers for the

Shreveport Times

Jefferson Journal

Jefferson Jimplecute

Houston Post-Dispatch

Prescott Daily News

Texarkana Twentieth Century

Capt. George Todd

Nat Sharp

Will Hill Thomas

And as told by individuals who once lived in Jefferson and by many who are now living and those who lived in Jefferson during her palmy days.

JEFFERSON

"From the region of the Upper Trinity and the headwaters of the Sabine, each traveler tells us, as he passes, some new tale of how the wilderness is falling under the axe of the builders of habitations and opening up of the earth."

"The town of Jefferson, in the Southern division of our country, was but yesterday a mere name upon paper and now we are told, quite a number of buildings are going up—several persons will have goods there directly. It is a town destined to concentrate a large inland commercial business."

"Immigration from Europe is filling up the beautiful country in the far west."—Northern Standard, January 16th, 1854.

The above article was given through the courtesy of Lola M. Bell, assistant to Advisory Board of Texas Historians.

While Texas, this year of 1936 celebrates the Centennial of its independence from Mexican rule, two cities of Texas will attain the anniversary of their birth.

In 1836 the townsites of Houston, Texas, and Jefferson, Texas, were established, similarly on the banks of bayous. Houston, the largest of Southern ports today, was founded on Buffalo Bayou and Jefferson, Texas equally important as a center of trade and commerce during its brief reign in the days before and following the Civil War, was located on Cypress Bayou.

Jefferson is known as the "Old Time Metropolis of East Texas," and there is something pathetic about Jefferson's history.

In the days following the Civil War Jefferson had a population of 25,000. It was the trading point of East Texas, and all roads led to Jefferson.

A natural barrier in Red River backed water into Cypress Bayou to an extent that navigation was possible as far as Jefferson. Steamboats landed in Jefferson from New Orleans, La. and points on the Ohio and Mississippi Rivers. River traffic in Jefferson goes back as early as 1845. The city of Shreveport, La., was long considered the head of navigation on Red River and was for many years the depot of trade for the large scope of country tributary to Jefferson.

About the year 1850 it became known that steamboats could ascend farther into the interior and finally the extreme terminus of navigation was fixed at Jefferson and a large portion of the shipping was diverted from Shreveport. No other inland town of the State ever attained the importance in river shipping that came to Jefferson in the late 60's and early 70's. As the extreme terminus of navigation on the waters of Cypress Bayou, Jefferson ranked among the established cities of the State, being second only to Galveston.

Some of the most palatial steamboats on the western rivers, and there were palatial steamers in those days, plied between Jefferson and New Orleans. Among them were: The Danube, Bessie Warren, Red Cloud, Iron Cities, Koontz, John T. Moore and Lizzie Hopkins. The cabins were elegantly furnished and the furnishings surpassed those of the best hotels of the country. Each steamer carried an Italian band which played at the landings, during meals, for balls in the evening, or whenever wanted for the waltz or schottische. People dressed most elaborately in those days, both men and women. They carried immense trunks, with two or three compartments for hats alone. Suit cases were unknown. In the early days, large oil lamps with reflectors were used as headlights on the boats and pine knots supplied the illumination for the negro deckhands to see how to work. All boats carried signal lights in the smoke stacks, which could be seen from all directions. A red light on the left, a green light on the right, they were known as "Larboard" and "Starboard."

The deckhands could not read and in order to distribute freight a playing card was placed over the name of the towns, for instance, Marshall, Texas, was known as "King of Diamonds," Longview, Texas, as "Ace of Hearts" and Jefferson as "King of Spades." The deckhands were told the freight went to "King of Spades," etc., and a piece of freight was never known to get into the wrong place. The most troublesome of all freight to handle was mules.

The deckhands often worked 18 to 20 hours without rest. Their songs were known as "Coonjines." They had a haunting and somewhat barbaric quality and the harder the negroes worked the more they sang, keeping perfect time with their feet.

The captain's responsibility was great. He was responsible for the protection of life and property and the captains were often most heroic. Many captains on Red River never refused passage to anyone unable to pay, and their deeds have been recorded in history.

The largest steamers had a capacity of 6,000 bales of cotton.

While Jefferson was crowded with traffic, there were landings at practically all the big plantations on the Bayou and Lake. Some of the wharves at Jefferson were built by Thomas Hinkle, grandfather of Tom Hinkle of Paris, Texas, for whom is named Hinkle's Camp on Cypress Bayou, founded by Mr. Hinkle during the days of the Texas and Pacific railroad construction.

A few months before the Civil War the Legislature, under Governor Pease, passed a bill for an appropriation of some $200,000 to be used for the widening and deepening of the waterways of Texas. To Jefferson was allotted about $21,000 for a new turning basin and the general betterment of Big Cypress. The work was only partially completed when the war broke out and operations ceased.

As the war passed into its second year Red River became vitally important to the Federal Government because the Northern armies had not yet gained a foothold in that part of the country. After the capture of the forts below New Orleans, many of the Confederate ships fled to the safety and security of Red River and its tributaries.

During the Civil War the Confederate Government established a slaughter house, or packing plant, at Jefferson, through which to draw on Texas for a meat supply for the army. Cattle and sheep were slaughtered by the thousand and the dressed meat carried down to New Orleans, where it was reshipped to various branches of the army. The Federals sought to capture the meat supply of Texas but were defeated and the packing house continued to be operated until the end of the war.

In those days, before the railroads became a great factor in the country's development, the growth of a town with water transportation was deemed certain, and many of these supposedly fortunate towns scorned the railroads when they began to span the continent. Such was the attitude of Jefferson when the Texas and Pacific put through its main line from Texarkana westward.

At this time, about 1873, appeared Jay Gould upon the scene—the building genius of the Texas and Pacific railroad, seeking a right-of-way for his road. Meeting with a cool reception and failing in his attempt to get the right-of-way through Jefferson, he left the town in disgust and chagrin, making the somewhat prophetic statement that "Jefferson would see the day when bats would roost in its church belfries and grass grow in its streets." The Texas and Pacific, instead of going through the town, made a half circle to avoid it and today the station is small, unkempt, and a considerable distance from the town. Freight rates went high and some time after this the United States Government removed the natural dam that backed water up and made Big Cypress Bayou and the lakes navigable.

Jefferson in its early days had no money and did not need any. The women spun the wool, wove the cloth and made the clothes for the family. Shoes were paid for in hides.

As Jefferson grew, towns sprang up to the west, and there was a continual stream of wagons going and coming. Mrs. Spearman owned the toll bridge and Mr. G. E. Dalby then a mere lad, was employed by her at fifty cents a day to keep the bridge. He is said to have often taken in $60 and $70 a day in toll.

All the cotton raised in Louisiana, Southwestern Arkansas and North Texas was "wagoned" to Jefferson, and was often stacked up for six or seven miles out waiting to be weighed. The annual receipts exceeded 100,000 bales. Farmers would take nothing but silver and gold for their cotton. They had no faith in bank notes and greenbacks, except when they went to pay their taxes. Then they exchanged silver and gold for paper money which was worth only seventy-five cents on the dollar but was accepted at face value by the government.

[5]

The late Capt. W. R. White of Nevada is said to have been Jefferson's first merchant, while Bateman Bros. (King, Andy and Quincy) were the leading merchants and cotton buyers. When a farmer got his money for his cotton he received a gallon of whiskey free.

Jefferson in her palmiest days, is said to have had a population of 30,000. There was plenty of money and people seemed quite as anxious to pass it around as they were to get more, which spirit kept things moving.

EXCLUSIVE SOCIAL SET

Jefferson even boasted an exclusive social set, left over from the Southern Aristocracy of Ante Bellum days, and keeping up the customs in the steamboats and parlors of the city hotels, both of which were palatial in their appointments.

An example of a steamboat adveitisement follows:

REGULAR JEFFERSON AND NEW ORLEANS PACKET
For Shreveport

Grand   Grand
Bayou   Ecore

**St. Maurice, Cotile, Alexander, Norman's
Berrin's and Way Landings.**
Stand A No. 1 in all Insurance Companies

The Light Draught Passenger Steamer

LIZZIE HOPKINS
J. T. ROOT, Master
SAM LAWSON, Clerk

Will run between Jefferson, (Texas) and New Orleans, during the season.

For Freight or passengers, apply on board, Feb. 17, 1868.

STOCKADE

Just after the war between the States the town of Jefferson was thrown into panic by the murder one night of a "carpet bagger"—carpet bagger being the name given to those men who came into the Southern towns immediately following the war to stir up the people, and especially the negroes, against the authorities,—it was necessary for the government to send troops to Jefferson to restore order. A stockade was built on the hill called "Sand Town," this stockade was made of immense timbers, and was about 70x100 feet, with walls fifteen feet high and broad enough on top for the soldiers to walk constantly. Many prominent men of Jefferson were placed in this prison, where life was most cruel and unbearable. Many died from exposure and pneumonia.

[6]

Mr. Lev. Gray told us that he made just one visit to the stockade, going with his mother and Mrs. Slaughter. Just after leaving to go home Mr. Slaughter escaped. Mr. Slaughter had only one arm but he proved himself a fast runner. He made his way to the river and cast a stone across. The soldiers, hearing the noise and seeing the water disturbed, began searching for Mr. Slaughter on the other side, while he followed the bank of the river into the City and to Allen and Ligon Wholesale and Retail Grocery Store on Dallas Street. Major Allen hid him in the basement of the store. When the soldiers came to look for Mr. Slaughter and started down in the basement Major Allen said: "All right, but what if there is a bull dog down there?" The soldiers left immediately.

This is just one instance of many narrow escapes from the Stockade.

THE CORRAL

The Corral, now used as a swimming pool, and known to the young boys for years as the "swimming hole" was the barracks for the Federal Army and Infantry, which was later moved to San Antonio. The headquarters for Gen. Buell was situated on the corner, just across the Broadway railroad crossing, east of the Cypress Bottling Works.

CHIEF JUSTICE HAUGHN

Chief Justice Haughn came to Jefferson in the early days of Jefferson's history, with the backing of the U. S. Government to create discord between the white and colored population. He entered politics, after serving as Chief Justice a number of years, and became judge. He later had as his opponent for the office Judge S. W. Moseley who, regardless of the fact that every election box was compelled to have one negro to help in the election, was elected Nov. 22, 1882.

A political meeting was held in Kellyville, Texas, five miles west of Jefferson, which many from Jefferson attended, and among those was Chief Justice Haughn. After the meeting the men from Jefferson stayed for a short time to chat with friends but Chief Justice Haughn was not interested and left. When he reached what is now known as the old Freeman house, he was killed and his body was found in a deep ditch. Every manager of the election boxes was arrested, but to no avail, as it is not known today, in 1944, how or by whose hand he met death.

TEXAS' FIRST FEDERAL COURT

The first Federal Court to sit in the State of Texas met in Jefferson in 1879 with Judge Amos Morill on the bench. In a short time the court was made a circuit, which included San Antonio and Galveston.

Three generations of Jefferson men served succeeding terms as clerks of the court—W. E. Singleton, W. E. Singleton, Jr., and J. M. Singleton. These men served for a total of sixty years.

The first court met in the Post Office which had been established in 1842 and was located in the Northeast corner of Polk and Austin Streets, and was the only Federal building in Jefferson. All records were kept in this building and when word came that Federal troops would possibly come through Jefferson and that all valuable papers and documents should be moved to a spot further interior for safe keeping, local authorities hastily gathered the court records and sent them to Dallas from which place they had not been returned after 65 years—though efforts have been made to have them returned.

THE CITY OF JEFFERSON, TEXAS
as a
MANUFACTURING DISTRICT IN 1871

The undersigned would respectfully invite the attention of capitalists, at home and abroad, to the manufacturing facilities of the City of Jefferson and its surroundings, with a view of securing such co-operation as our railroad prospects and natural advantages seem to warrant. We say railroad prospects, because our city will shortly become the Great Railroad Center of Northeastern Texas. Here the International Trans-Continental and East Line and Red River Railroad will all intersect ere many more months elapse, thus opening up direct communications with all the leading business centers in the Union. So far as railroads are concerned, Jefferson will become the Atlanta of all that portion of the State known as "Northeastern Texas." Associated with this fact is another equally significant in a manufacturing point of view. We have here within striking distance inexhaustible supplies of material for the manufacture on an extensive scale of an endless variety of articles; and for steam purposes we have living waters and fuel in abundance. Indeed Nature has here strewn upon the earth's surface and planted beneath it forests and mines immeasureable in extent and of inestimable value.

Before proceeding, however, to detail the manner in which these should be utilized, we should invite attention to a few particulars respecting the

CITY OF JEFFERSON

The City of Jefferson is yet in its infancy. But a few short years have passed since the ground on which it stands was a wilderness, but its growth has been rapid and substantial. It now numbers not less than 12,000 inhabitants, and the business houses being constructed of brick, it wears an air of solidity, such as is seldom seen in this State. Its Churches and many of its private residences are unsurpassed in the State, in points of taste and elegance and its business men are quite as enterprising as those of any other city within the confines of the Empire State of Texas.

Jefferson has already a National Bank, a Citizens Savings Bank and three private Banks, but such is the extent of her trade even this number has not been found sufficient, and a charter has been secured for another National Bank, which will soon go into operation. She also has a Chamber of Commerce, an iron foundry and Machine Shop, several planing mills, sash door and blind Factories, the National Cotton Compress Company etc. and here, too, is located the East Texas State Agricultural, Mechanical and Stock Raising Association.

The exports from the City of Jefferson, for the year ending September 1st, 1886 were not less than 25,000 bales of cotton; for the year ending September 1st, 1872, the exports were: Cotton (bales) 76,328; Dry hides 84,762, Green Hides 18,471; Wool (Lbs.) 87,623; Peltries 48,210; Bois d'arc Seeds, (bushels) 9,721; Cattle 5,381; Sheep 821; Lumber (feet) 121,000.

The Steamboat arrivals for the same period were 226, with a carrying capacity of from 225 to 700 tons each.

Being situated at the head of navigation, on Big Cypress Bayou, a port necessitated by reason of the immovable raft, which long since formed in Red River, above this point: heretofore Jefferson, has been compelled to rely on water transportation; it is, therefore, with a great degree of satisfaction that she witnesses the movements on foot to make her a great railroad center. When her facilities for transportation are thus increased, no town in Northern or Eastern Texas will have a brighter future, or greater commercial advantages. For a long time past this city has transacted more business annually than any city in Texas, with the single exception of Galveston. What then will be her capacity when the above named railroads all come to her aid?

JEFFERSON AS A MANUFACTURING DISTRICT

But great as our city is as a commercial center she will yet develop other and more important interests, and that too within a limited period of time for it has been demonstrated to the entire satisfaction of all capitalists, who have given their attention to the matter that there is not in the whole south a district which combines so many advantages for manufacturing on an intensive scale, such an endless variety of articles as the city under consideration & the country immediately surrounds it. In support of this statement let us descend to particulars:

There is, for instance, within the immediate neighborhood of our city more iron ore than can be consumed in centuries, and this ore is richer than any other yet known in the United States. Six miles from the center of Jefferson are iron hills towering above the surrounding country which alone will yield an inexhaustible supply of ore and, this ore is richer and more easily worked than that found in Missouri's famous "Iron Mountain." But the whole country contains more or less ore of this character, and here, where the raw material is so abundant, and water and fuel for steam purposes so readily procured, and transportation by railroads

[9]

and by water so accessible, there can be erected furnaces, forges and foundries that would successfully compete with any now in existence in this country. Already the largest iron foundry in this state is in operation four miles from the city, and two miles this side of the iron hills of which we have spoken; and this foundry—G. A. Kelly's at Kellyville is manufacturing on an extensive scale cooking stoves and heating stoves that are unsurpassed by any imported to this market, either in beauty and finish or in quality, and the plow manufactured by this establishment is pronounced by all those who are using it—and a large number are now in use—to be equal in all respects to the Hall and Speer or Avery plow, and much more durable by reason of the superior quality of our iron. Such is the demand for the products of this foundry the owner is now seeking to increase his manufacturing facilities by organizing a joint Stock Company, with a capital of $200,000, as nothing short of this amount will enable him to fill his orders in the future.

Again 20 miles from this city, and adjacent to the route of the East Line and Red River Railway, we come to a vein of copper ore, impregnated with both gold and silver. This ore in the hands of the assayer has been found to be very pure, quite as much as any in the South, not excepting that from the Wichita country. The supply is by no means limited. In fact its limits have no. as yet been ascertained. In that vicinity, also, as well as in many other sections within striking distance of this city by rail as soon as the projected roads are completed, there is a great abundance of cannel coal of a fine quality. Manufacturers will comprehend at a glance the significance of this fact, and know how to appreciate it. That there is coal enough of this character for all local manufacturing purposes there is no doubt.

No section of country that can be named offers a better quality or a greater variety of timber for building and manufacturing purposes than that in the immediate vicinity of the City of Jefferson. For building we have, in the greatest abundance, the very best of pine, black-walnut, gum, white-oak and cypress; for manufacturing, we have not only the above named but also hickory, cedar, Bois d'arc, etc. The quality of our pine and oak is unsurpassed North or South and at the Mills as good a quality of black-walnut as one could desire can be had in any quantity for $2.00 per hundred feet; contrast that with the prices paid in the North, and West and the advantage we possess will be appreciated. For the manufacture of wagons we have an unlimited supply of hickory. Bois d'arc and white oak within striking distance and for wooden ware we have all the oak, cedar and cypress we need.

Going west, along the line of the Texas and Pacific Railway, we soon come to those immense prairies, whose settlers must rely, during our day at least, on other sections for their building materials, wagon materials, furniture and wooden ware, and everything else which requires timber in its construction. Right here, then at this end of that great thoroughfare, we should and must manufacture ready-fitted timbers for building, including shingles, sash doors, and blinds and every other article needed in the construction of houses as well as furniture and wooden ware for the same. We say ready-fitted timbers because these can be prepared by machinery, like sash doors and blinds, in a better manner and at much less expense than on prairies, and the purchaser will then only pay the freight on what he actually uses. That is he will not be taxed for freight on waste materials.

This brings us to the natural conclusion that here, where, the materials are in their native state, should be the manufactories. That is here should be the saw mills, the planing mills, the shingle machines, machinery for the manufacture of ready made houses, furniture, wagon and wooden ware manufactories, etc. Besides, here too, where we have the iron and the white oak and the hickory we should manufacture every kind of agricultural implement our State requires. There is no earthly reason why we should import these—why others in their manufacture should falter at our expense. We have all the requisites all the essentials right here at home; let us avail ourselves of them.

Then again, why are our hides sent abroad to be tanned and then returned to us at our expense while our forests in this vicinity at least, abound, in red oak bark? Can any one assign one good and valid reason why this is done? Have we not room for tanyards. If so, let us construct them and exhibit our good sense in tanning our hides at home, and then instead of paying Massachusetts and other States for manufacturing our boots and shoes let us do this ourselves. When we learn to act instead of employing others to act for us, then, and not till then will we become independent.

Here, too, we should without delay erect Cotton and Woolen Mills, Cotton Seed oil mills, Cotton gin and Cotton press manufactories, where nothing is required but capital, labor and enterprise

There is no reason why a broom, or a harness, or saddle, or a horse-collar, or a carriage of any description, or a pump or a chair, or a barrel, or a single article of furniture should be imported into Texas. We, therefore, invite capitalists at home and abroad to unite their means with ours and assist us in manufacturing what we have enumerated and other necessities of life. We have the locality for doing this in a preeminent degree, & hence the invitation is here extended.

In this connection we should invite the special attention of boat-builders to the fact that at Potter's Point on Fairy Lake—or "Ferry Lake," as it is sometimes called—15 miles from this city is one of the most desirable places in the South for a Dock-yard. In that vicinity there is an abundance of white oak and other suitable timber for the construction of Steamboats, and right here all the necessary machinery could be manufactured, and forwarded by water navigation to that point. In the construction of boats on the shore of that lake there would be no loss of time by reason of the severity of the weather not even during the winter time, as in yards further North Our climate would greatly favor such an enterprise in that locality

The above suggestions are offered for the consideration of capitalists everywhere, and we would add that there is a disposition among our people to extend a hearty welcome to all who assist us in developing our natural resources. Lands for manufacturing purposes can here be had in healthy localities for a reasonable consideration, and the privilege of mining can here be had for nothing by way of encouragement to capitalists. Our section is as healthy as any in the wide world,—no epidemic ever prevailed here—and those who desire to make their home in our midst will find this section as pleasant as any in the State, and the society one in which strangers would soon feel at home.

Before closing we would remark that the Legislature of this State during the winter of 1871, passed an act exempting from taxation of all kinds, for a period of five years, all machinery introduced into the State for the manufacture of cotton and wool, and that act is still in force; also that during the same session—see General Laws of Texas, of 12th Legislature, 2nd Session, Chapter ixxx,—a general incorporation act was passed. During this session a special act was also passed and approved Dec 2nd, 1871, incorporating the "Texas Manufacturing Company." Four of the incorporators were and three still are inhabitants of this city. Here also is the headquarters of this company.

Any further information Capitalists or Manufacturers may desire respecting this locality will be cheerfully furnished by the undersigned.

Respectfully Yours,

L. T. GRAY, Mayor of Jefferson City.
A. G. CLOPTON, M. D., President Chamber of Commerce.
CAPT. J. M. DeWARE, Chief of Police, Jefferson.
MASON & CAMPBELL, Lawyers.
MOSELEY & SPARKS, Attorneys and Land Agents.
CRAWFORD & CRAWFORD, Attorneys at Law.
EPPERSON & MAXEY, Attorneys at Law.
PENN & TODD, Lawyers.
M. F. MOORE, Attorney at Law.
REEVES & WORD, Attorneys at Law
THOMAS J. HUDSON, Attorney at Law
R. DeJERNETT, Physician and Surgeon.
L S. RAYFIELD, Physician and Surgeon
G. H. WOOTTEN, Physician
S. EASON, Physician and Surgeon.
A. P. BROWN, Physician and Surgeon.
A. A. TERHUNE, Physician and Surgeon.
NATIONAL BANK, W. M. Harrison, President.
CITIZENS SAVINGS BANK, W. Q. Bateman, President Jno M. Lewis, Cashier.

JAMES ARBUCKLE & CO., Bankers.

J. A. NORSWORTHY & COX, Bankers.

ERASTUS JONES, Banker.

GRAHAM & TAYLOR, Receiving, Forwarding and Commission Merchants

GOYNE, HARPER & MURPHY, Receiving, Forwarding and Commission Merchants.

A. GILHAM, Receiving, Forwarding and Commission Merchants.

MIDDLEBROOKS & WALL, Receiving, Forwarding and Commission Merchants.

A. C. ALLEN, Receiving, Forwarding and Commission Merchant.

RUSSELL, RAINEY and CO., Wholesale Grocers and Commission Merchants.

ELLIS BAGBY and CO., Wholesale Grocers and Commission Merchants.

BATEMAN & BRO., Wholesale Grocers and Commission Merchants.

BOGEL & RIDDLE, Wholesale Grocers and Commission Merchants.

NORWOOD & SCOTT, Commission Merchants.

S. FRANKLE, Commission Merchant.

BELL & ROBINSON, Commission Merchants, and Real Estate Agents.

TORRANS & RIVES, Commission Merchants and Cotton Buyers.

B. J. TERRY, Cotton·F ctor.

WAYLAND & WHATLEY, Wholesale Grocers.

JG FELLNER, JR., Wholesale Grocer.

COLLINS, EPPERSON & EZELL, Wholesale Grocers.

T. J. ROGERS, Wholesale Grocer.

BARNS & ELLINGTON, Wholesale Grocers.

F. ROBINSON, Wholesale Grocer.

F. C. BAKER, Wholesale Grocer.

JNO. A. FIELDER, Grocer and Importer of Fancy Goods.

J. M. MURPHY, Grocer and General Merchandise.

O. C. HERRENKIND, Retail Grocer.

NANCE & MODRALL, Retail Grocers.

E. MARX, General Merchandise, Wholesale.

P. ELDRIDGE & BRO., General Merchandise.

MOORING & LYON, General Merchandise.

K. MEYER, General Merchandise.

BIRGE, NICKOLS & CO., Dry Goods, Wholesale.

JAMES HOBAN, Dry Goods.

F. A. SCHLUTER & SON, Dry Goods, Staple and Fancy.

SIMS & NORRIS, Dry Goods.

S. W. STONE, Hardware Merchant.

JOHN C. KOLTER & CO., Hardware Merchants.

R. BALLAUF & CO., Hardware Merchants.

BONEY & BROOKS, Druggist, Wholesale and Retail.

E. W. TAYLOR, Druggist and Bookseller

W. J. SEDBERRY, Druggist and Bookseller.

BRADFORD, BRIDGE & CO, Furniture and Carriages.

J. BRUCKMULLER, Furniture Dealer.

W. H. WYMAN, Furniture Manufacturer and Dealer.

RUFUS MUSE & CO., Wholesale Dealer in Liquors, Tobacco and Cigars.

TAYLOR & PINSON, Agricultural Implements and Machinery.

R. MAN WARING, Real Estate Owner.

DOPPLEMAYER & EBERSTADT, Real Estate Owners.

NEY & BRO., Real Estate Owners

V. H. CLAIRBORNE, Real Estate Owner

WARD TAYLOR, Real Estate Owner

W. C. BAKER, Real Estate Owner.

L. MOODY, Real Estate Owner.

R. TOWERS, Property Owner.

T. G. ANDERSON, General Insurance Agent.

COTTON BROS, General Insurance Agents.

FRANK O SETH, General Agent, Universal Life Insurance Company.

GILBERT & CO, Agents for Capitalists and Manufacturers.

J. A H HOSACK, Auctioneer and Real Estate Broker.

W. H. JOHNSON, District Clerk and Notary Public.

W. E. KNEELAND, Notary Public

EDWARD GUTHERIDGE, Deputy District Clerk and Notary Public.

J. OPPENHEIMER, Recorder and Collector of City of Jefferson.

S. A. THOMPSON, Boot and Shoe Manufacturer and Dealer.

LAWRENCE & REATON. Crockery, China and Glassware.

J. H CARLIN, Merchant Tailor.

HUGO FOX, Manufacturer of Candies.

J. B. TULLIS, Surgeon Dentist

ADAM STOLL, Butcher

G. A. KELLY, Proprietor Kelly's Foundry.

MORRIS, McKEOWN & CO, Proprietors of Foundry and Machine Manufactory.

E. W. MORTEN, Proprietor "National Cotton Compress."

TRICE STEWART & CO., Proprietors Jefferson Planing Mill.

J B. LIGON, Building Contractor.

CRUMP & HUNSUCKER, Builders.

C. F. L. SMITY, Civil and Mechanical Engineer.

J. M. TUCKER, Alderman.

GEO. W. ROBERTS, Supt. Jefferson Chamber of Commerce.

CAPT. W. H. COIT, Principal Coit's Military and Commercial Academy.

ROOTS & HYNSON, Railroad Contractors.

[14]

JEFFERSON DEMOCRAT, Miller, McEachern and Alexander Proprietors, J. B. McEachern Editor.

"JEFFERSON TIMES," R. W. Loughery, Editor and Proprietor.

J. C. ROGERS & CO., Printers, Lithographers, Wholesale and Retail Books, Stationery, Blank Books, etc.

ARTIFICIAL GAS

In making history—the first artificial gas plant in Texas started at Jefferson, the gas being made from rich pine and pine knots, which were cut and placed in iron drums called "retorts." These retorts were about seven feet long, tapering off at one end like the mouth of a jug. The bottom was opened with a door which securely fastened the pine inside. The retorts were subject to intense heat, the steamlike substance which exuded from the pine during the heating process escaped through an opening in the top and into the iron mains or pipes, through which it was conveyed over the business section of town—to ornamental hollow posts, on top of which were large globes. These were lighted at night and turned off in the mornings. Water often accumulated in the pipes and a negro would remove it with a hand pump—this frequently took most of the day.

The gas was forced through the mains by a large drum affair raised during the day and at night gradually sinking, its weight forcing the gas through the pipes. The large foundation upon which this drum rested is still standing near the business part of town, and several of the "retorts" may be seen in various parts of town. These "retorts" have been donated for war purposes.

Mr. J. M. Thomas, known as " Gas House Thomas," was sole owner and operator.

JEFFERSON HAD FIRST ARTIFICIAL ICE

Tradition, and a sworn statement, before a notary public, by the late Mr. B. J. Benefield, an honored citizen of Jefferson, gives to Jefferson, Texas, the honor of having had within its city limits the first artificial ice plant in the United States and many say in the world.

Old settlers claim that it was in operation in the late 60's but Mr. Benefield places the date at 1874 or '75 because he returned to Marion County from Red River County in 1874 and began working for Boyle and Scott, as the first dispenser of artificial ice, using his own wagon and teams, and sold the ice for ten cents per pound. He states that the ice was made in cakes four or five feet long, two or three feet in width and one inch thick.

The plant continued in operation about one year, when Mr. Boyle, who was the originator of the idea that artificial ice could be made, went north in search of some one to finance the making of the product.

Mr. J. E. Hasty says that Mr. Boyle raised money before he went north, to finance his project but he was never heard of after he left and his partner, Henry Scott, went into bankruptcy, while someone else profited by their pioneer efforts.

Old citizens of the state say that the plant was moved to Harrisburg, Texas, near Houston, at the time Mr. Boyle went north.

One incident remaining clear to Mr. Benefield was that one of his customers, a prominent citizen, bought one thousand pounds of ice and placed it in his cistern so that he and his family might have an unlimited supply of ice water through the summer. However, the experiment failed, of course, and the man remained a daily customer of Mr. Benefield.

It was Mr. Benefield's understanding that the machine was patented in the U. S. Patent office.

The gas used in the manufacturing of the ice was made at the plant and the machinery was run by steam power. The old site of the plant is within the City Limits, just beyond Willard Hill on Highway 49.

Mr. Henry Scott, one of the founders, has a son and daughter now living in Dallas.

At a meeting of the Southwestern Ice Association on December 3rd., 1926, Mr. F. R. Senor presented a motion, which was accepted by the Association, the erection of a memorial in Jefferson to the honor of the man and place where the first artificial ice was manufactured in the U. S. However, that monument has never been erected.

CHURCHES

EPISCOPAL CHURCH

On June 8th., 1860 the friends of the Protestant Episcopal Church held a meeting in the Cumberland Presbyterian place of worship for the purpose of organizing an Episcopal congregation. Bishop Alex Gregg, D. D. was called to the chair and E. G. Benners appointed secretary, the Rev. E. A. Wagner being present, the secretary read the articles of association which had been prepared in accordance with the canons.

Signed by:

E. G. Benners	Helen Benners
Abbie Foscue	Amanda M. Winslow
Adeline G. Pitkins	W. I. C. Rogers
I. Winslow	Orville Yerger
Virginia Yerger	A. M. Walker
Jennie E. Duke	Alexander Starr
Emmer Charlotte Cox	Martha Murphy
Virginia Todd	H. Witherspoon

Services were held in the Cumberland Presbyterian Church, Freemans Hall, and private homes until 1886 when the new church was completed. Bishop Gregg was the first clergyman to preach in the new church and Rev. E. G. Benners the first minister in charge.

Members of the first vestry were: E. G. Benners, Orville Yerger,

[16]

John Winslow, Dr A M. Walker, Dr W. C Rogers, Dr. H. Witherspoon, H. H. Black, and Judge W S Todd.

At one time the church was badly damaged by storm and Dr. D. Guinn, who was minister in charge at the time, remodeled the church using the old building as a foundation. It was made into a beautiful brick veneer building

PRESBYTERIAN CHURCH

The Cumberland Presbyterian Church in Jefferson was organized between 1846 and 1850 by Rev. Solomon Awalt, who lived many years in the Pine Tree neighborhood, three miles from Longview, Texas, an old fashioned Cumberland Presbyterian preacher. He was a German, a diligent bible student and a strong theologian.

The first church was a small frame building located on the corner of Line and Jefferson Streets. In 1873 the brick church was built by Mr. John Ligon, on Jefferson Street. It was at that time the finest Cumberland Presbyterian Church in Texas. Dr. N. P. Modrall was the first minister in charge of the New Church. The 1875 general assembly met in the church. After the assembly the railroads of Texas gave all the delegates from other states a free excursion over Texas, visiting Dallas, Houston, Galveston and other places of interest. This beautiful church is still standing and in constant use. It is known as the Presbyterian Church U. S. A.

The Presbyterians Manse of today known to many of the "old timers" as "The old General Rogers Place" is said to be the oldest home in Jefferson, and is in good repair today. At the corner of this ancient building is found an old iron post, with a large wheel design near the center, which is as placed there in the early days of Jefferson. Then the most direct route to the boat landing was along that street, turning this corner and passing down Delta Street, the oxen trains cut the corner so close that some protection had to be given the property. And today the post hangs far out over the street as a result of the oxen running too close.

Most of this information was given by Rev. W. B. Preston, who served the church twice, from June 1888 to December 1890, and from February 1910 to December 1911.

THE FIRST BAPTIST CHURCH

The 24th. day of March 1855 the first Baptist Church of Jefferson was organized. The first addition to the church after it organized was William I. Bateman in June 1855. The deed to the church lots where the church now stands were recorded Oct. 11th. 1860.

The first conference after the war was Jan. 28th., 1866 with Rev. H. T. Buckner presiding. Rev. Buckner was known later as "Father Buck-

[17]

ner" to his 800 orphan children, who loved him devotedly. He made Buckner's Orphans Home the largest and most noted in Texas. W. E. Penn and wife came to Jefferson from Lexington, Tenn. and on February 24th, 1886 joined the first Baptist church Major Penn immediately became superintendent of the Sunday School, continuing in this capacity for ten years. He was known in 1877 as "The famous state Evangelist of Texas". In 1866 a committee was appointed to solicit contributions to build a church. W E. Penn and B J. Terry were the first building committee, this resulted in the brick edifice which is today standing on Polk Street. The church was dedicated Dec. 4th. 1869. Rev. D. B. Hale (grandfather of Jim, Miss May Belle Hale and Mrs Oralee Hale Miller) assisting in the dedication service.

In 1870 a pipe (imitation) organ was installed costing $1,000.00. The organ remained in use for fifty years. Rev. C. P. McCloud was the first pastor of the First Baptist church in 1869, while the Rev. D. B. Culbertson, father of Col. D. B. Culbertson, acted as pastor while the church was using the Presbyterian and Methodist churches in which to worship. Dr. Tucker was pastor when the church was first organized and he received $200 for his services during the year of 1855. The Southern Baptist convention met with this church May 7th., 1874 and was the largest ever held up to this time and first to meet in the state of Texas. Over 1000 attended. Many distinguished divines were present including Dr. A. J Broadus, Dr. J. R. Graves, P. H. Mall, J. L. Burrour, W. W. Laundrum and many others. W. W. Laundrum, Jr. was ordained as a minister during the convention. His father delivered the charge. The convention held until May 12th. when the visitors were taken on a free tour of the state of Texas, through the courtesy of the Texas and Pacific Railroad.

In January, 1877, J. H. Rowell, Sr., was elected superintendent of the Sunday School, a position he held about thirty years.

Rev. S. A. Hayden was pastor of the First Baptist Church for five years, he was given leave of absence in 1882 to visit Europe and the Holy Land. In 1883 he resigned to take possession of the Texas Baptist, at Dallas. Dr. L. J. Anderson, father of Mrs. Jodie Rowell, was another much beloved pastor during the latter years of the church. Plans are at present being rushed to repair the building, preserving the original exterior architecture.

JEFFERSON METHODIST CHURCH SOUTH

Pastors

The first Methodist preacher to be appointed to Jefferson was the Reverend James W Baldridge. The year was 1844. That Methodist preachers had preached in Jefferson prior to this date is very likely. The great and wide-spread Harrison Circuit covered this country and, in all likelihood, the modest settlement which sprang up at the head of navigation was a preaching point for the circuit rider

The Rev. Mr Baldridge had joined the conference in 1843. He served Jefferson for three years the records state. Jefferson was in the East Texas Conference as an appointment the first year that conference was formed from the older Texas Conference. Later in 1867, the church was in the North Texas Conference, and in still more recent years, the territory came back into the Texas Conference.

At the close of the year 1845 the church reported 50 white and 3 colored members The custom of having the slaves join the church was continued through Civil War days. By 1845 a number of churches had grown up through the immediate country about Jefferson, so the work was listed as the Jefferson Circuit with the town as the principal church. The membership reported that year was 508 whites and 89 colored.

A complete record of all pastors for Jefferson from 1855 to the present day is preserved. The names of some from the years 1847 to 1855 are missing.

The Famous Bell

Legend held dear in Jefferson says that in the year 1854 the famous Meneley Bell Foundry of Troy, N. Y., was called upon to cast a silver bell for the Methodist Church. To assure a silvery tone, 1500 Mexican silver dollars were raised and sent to the foundry to be melted down and cast into the bell. That bell hangs in the belfry of the Methodist Church today.

Some of the present citizens of Jefferson tell that the 1500 silver dollars were the gift of one man, famous and beloved in this section, Mr. F. A. Schluter, and that the date was 1858 since that is the date on the bell.

The bell was brought by water down the Ohio and Mississippi rivers to New Orleans, then back up the Mississippi and Red Rivers to Shreve--port and .through Caddo Lake and the Cypress to Jefferson.

The Church Buildings

The Methodist Church building entered into the early history of Jefferson. In the early days a private school was taught in the basement. Some existing records of the Jefferson Baptist Church point out that the preaching services of the Baptist were held "in the Methodist Church."

Possibly in the years of prosperity of the '50's a fine brick building is revealed in the remarkable "bird's-eye-view" picture of Jefferson which is preserved in the Carnegie Library. It took its place with the magnificent structures which had been erected by the Presbyterians and Baptists in this same period—the "fair fifties". The Methodist building was con-demned some fifty years ago, razed and a new wooden structure built, using a part of the original foundation of the brick building That wooden building is the existing Methodist Church of today Thus Jefferson Methodism has probably seen three buildings in its over 90 years of history

Great Meetings

In 1860 the East Texas Conference met in Jefferson on October 24-30 A half dozen young preachers were admitted on trial at this session who were to go out and make history in the state and church Among these was one, John H. McLean, who served in Jefferson for two years, (being sent to Jefferson in 1863) and who in 1874 and 1875 served as Presiding Elder of the Marshall District, of which Jefferson was a station. He became an influential figure in Texas Methodism and education.

There was excitement in Jefferson and Texas in those October days over the national presidential election. Portents of civil conflicts were plentiful, and when news that Abraham Lincoln had been elected President reached Jefferson during the conference session, many declared that it meant WAR!

When the next session of an Annual Conference met in Jefferson ten years later (1870) Jefferson was in the North Texas Conference, the Civil War having come and gone. But its effects very present. Some of the honored names of 1860 were missing Among these was the name of Rev. W. B. Hill who was pastor in Jefferson during 1860. He was killed at Fort Donelson in 1862.

Gifts to the Church Now Recalled

Property

The first title to property on which to build a church was granted in 1848. The first church evidently stood in property to which the church did not hold title Mr. Allen Urquhart "sold" (the $100.00 of the transaction seems to have been given by Mr. Urquhart) to the Trustees of the Methodist Episcopal Church, South, in the town of Jefferson the lot on which the present church stands. Construction of the brick church must have started shortly, for many older residents of Jefferson today state that "the Methodist Church was the first church in town."

Mrs. Mamie Tullis Smith remembers hearing a former slave of her father tell how her father put him to work wheeling brick and mortar and how tired he became. He spoke, however, of what a great honor to him it was to work on the Methodist Church.

The lots on which the parsonage was later built were acquired in 1866. One lot was purchased for $100.00 from a Mr. and Mrs. Rooks. The second was "purchased" from Mr. F. A. Schluter for $500.00, the money being given by Mr. Schluter himself. It was this honored resident and pioneer Methodist who served as one of the trustees in 1848 when the church lot was acquired and who gave the whole $1500.00 in Mexican silver dollars to go into the bell. Mr. J. C. Murphy, a wholesaler with a great business, likewise served on this Board of Trustees, and it was he who carried the dollars on a steamer to New Orleans for shipment to New York.

The Gas Heating System

There is a bronze plate hanging on the wall of the church with the following inscription:

THE GAS HEATING EQUIPMENT
IN THIS CHURCH
WAS GIVEN
BY
MISS BERTIE TAYLOR
IN MEMORY OF
HER BROTHER
WARD TAYLOR

On the opposite wall rests this inscription:

THE ELECTRIC FANS
IN THIS CHURCH
WERE GIVEN
BY
D. WURTSBAUGH
IN MEMORY OF
HIS WIFE
MRS. LUVENIA CLEMENTINE WURTSBAUGH

This last year (1935) Miss Bertie Taylor turned over to the church for safe keeping a copy of the "First Directory of the Jefferson Methodist Episcopal Church, South, Jefferson Station, Marshall District, East Texas Conference. This directory was compiled in 1896 by the following Directory Committee:

L. S. Schluter.	R. B. Walker.
W. C. Hill.	W. P. Schluter.
John Grant.	D. M. Smith.
O. P. Thomas, Presiding Elder	
G. V. Ridley, Pastor.	

It contains a letter to the membership from the pastor, lists of former pastors, presiding elders, bishops, lists of the Official Boards, ushers, assessments, order of church worship and roll of the membership.

It is impossible to include all the many gifts to a church from every faithful and unselfish member and friend of the church. Gifts of service are continuous and do not stand out as these single ones.

The Organ

In the basement of the Methodist Church is the Sunday School Organ given in memory of little F. A. Schluter, only child of Mr. W. P. and Mrs.

[21]

A. L. Schluter. F. A. died at Hughes Springs on August 21, 1892 at the age of 8 years. By adding to the savings their son had kept over a period of time, Mr. and Mrs. Schluter bought the organ to be used in the basement for Sunday School. The gift was most probably made in 1892 or 1893. Several Jeffersonians say that the gift was made shortly after the child's death.

ROMAN CATHOLIC CHURCH OF JEFFERSON, TEXAS
IMMACULATE CONCEPTION

In April 1866 James M. Murphy and Allen Urquhart of Jefferson, Texas, donated, for the purpose of building a Catholic Church and school, to Bishop Claudius M. Dubuis, Catholic Bishop, of Galveston, Texas, lots 10-11-12 in block 29, Urquhart division, said lots fronting 50 feet on Polk street and 150 on LaFayette street. These lots are where Sedberry's store now stands.

The contract for building the church was given, by Rev. J. M. Giraud, a Catholic priest, to Mr. Benard Whitkorn of Nacogdoches, Texas. He was assisted by George Whitkorn and Tony Hillenkamp and the building was completed in 1869.

In 1870 William H. Ward deeded lots 10-11-12, block 28 on LaFayette and Vale streets to Rev. J. M. Giraud and the church was moved to this location, where it now stands.

Rev. J. M. Giraud is supposed to have assisted in the moving of the church.

In 1870 the Catholic Sisters of Charity from Maryland had a Catholic school at the corner of Henderson and Market streets. In 1875 the Hebrew congregation appointed a committee to consider buying the Catholic school building, the committee being composed of H. Goldberg, L. Goldberg J. Weinstein, P. Eldridge, Joe Ney, A. Rosenthal, and I. Lewis. This committee appointed a committee to represent the Hebrew Sinai Congregation consisting of E. Mark, L. Goldberg, A. Rosenthal, and E Eberstadt, to purchase the property, which they did, including lots, buildings, and furniture.

The sisters of Charity of Maryland was represented by R. Ballauf. The property is still owned by the Hebrew Sinai Congregation and is in excellent condition.

The Catholics later built a two story frame building on Vale Street adjoining the church.

The building is now used as an apartment house, the school having been discontinued many years ago.

EXCELSIOR'S HISTORY

The northern end of the hotel, of frame construction, was built in the late fifties by Captain William Perry, from New Hampshire.

Captain Perry was killed, through mistaken identity, by a Yankee soldier as Captain Perry was standing on the corner near his home.

Captain Perry's daughter, Lucy, is said to have been the first child born in Jefferson, and was the first native Jeffersonian to be married there. She was married to Captain Claiborne, and to them were born four children, Perry, Howard, Fannie, and Lucylee. Captain and Mrs. Claiborne spent all of their married life in Jefferson, and the home place is still in excellent condition.

The Excelsior Hotel was originally known as the Irvine House and in 1871 was operated by Mr. A. Britton. Mrs. Kate Wood acquired it about 1877, and at her death the property was left jointly to Mr. George Niedermeier and her daughter, Mrs. Neeley. The present proprietors are Mr. and Mrs Walter Neidermeier

The old record books show the signatures of many noted men, among who were Jacob Astor, June 30, 1878, W. H Vanderbilt in 1881, Gen. Grant, Feb 7, 1881.

Near the top of a crowded column of signatures is the name of Jay Gould At the bottom of the page, in the same handwriting, is the notation "The end of Jefferson, Texas."

An old advertisement of the Irvine Hotel appears in the 1871 directory and states: "Stages arrive at and depart from this hotel daily."

The Post Office

The property on which the Post Office and Federal Courthouse now stand was donated by Mrs. Kate Wood, once owner of the hotel.

Today the hotel is noted for the many beautiful pieces of antique furniture. Among them is a "button bed", a suite in carved walnut, old fashioned secretary, settees, marble topped tables, quaint lamps, a massive Chickering square piano and its stool with needlepoint upholstery, and many lovely pictures, one worked in wool, valued at $1,000

For each table in the spacious dining hall there was a revolving silver castor with the various glass bottles for pepper and salt, vinegar, pepper sauce and catsup.

"Queen Mab"

In 1877 Jefferson gave a celebration in imitation of Mardi Gras, as put on at New Orleans, Louisiana, but called it "Queen Mab", borrowing the conception from Shakespeare, with those plays even frontiersmen and pioneers were familiar. The street parade was several miles in extent, made up of floats decorated with flowers and grotesques, carrying innumerable fairy folk and punctuated with bands of music with "Queen Mab" herself as central figure, the whole "blow out" winding up with a grand ball. This was an annual affair for many years.

Dr. George T. Veal of Dallas, Texas, tells us that far back in slavery times Jefferson was one of the most famed towns of the South, and was set down in the school geographies as the "Emporium of the Southwest."

Jefferson has truly lived up to its slogan, "Queen of the Cypress." Many visitors come from Dallas, Fort Worth, and even El Paso and many other towns to enjoy the fishing and hunting that can be found in the pine woods and lakes surrounding the historic old town

An Advertisement of a famous old hotel operated here:

THE HAYWOOD HOUSE

Jefferson, Texas

Largest and Finest Hotel Building West of the Mississippi

Has been fitted up in a style of elegance and comfort, that entitles it to the patronage of the home and traveling public. The rooms are comfortable, and have new furniture. The table supplied with the best the market affords, and the servants attentive. In a word it is the business of the Proprietors to consult the comfort of guests, and to make the house a desirable stopping place.

TERMS

Board and lodging, per month, payable weekly	$10.00
Without lodging, per month, payable weekly, advance	$ 7.50
Transient customers, per week	$15.00
Transient customers, per day	$ 3.00
Single Meal	$ 1.00

W. T. RIVES, Proprietor, Jefferson, Texas

The annex to the Haywood Home is the present home of Mrs. Lizzie Haywood.

McDonald's Machine Shop

In the machine man's history of Jefferson, the story is incomplete without the mention of what is now the Jefferson Foundry and Machine Shop, a descendant of one of the community's enterprises, now owned and operated by E. B. McDonald.

The original machine shop was Miles and Co., and its beginning about 1870. Morris and McKeoun followed as the new steps in the ladder of the Foundry's ownership.

M Bower acquired Morris' interest in the business and the name became McKeoun and Bower, later McKeoun and Lione and finally Mc-Keoun became sole owner.

The foundry burned in 1890 and the same year the McDonald Shop started its career. G. B. McDonald, father of E. B., John and George started the business with the help of his three sons, all of whom became noted machinists in East Texas

Mr McDonald came to Jefferson, Texas, in 1886 and operated a flour mill and later had charge of the City gas system.

When the boys were old enough and trained as machinists, Mr. Mc-

Donald went into the machine shop and foundry and together they built a business which is considered one of the most complete machine shops in East Texas.

The present owner, E. B. McDonald is considered an authority on much of Jefferson and Marion County history. He is a hobbyist of note and collects authentic markers of the country's history.

His ability is accepted with a note of finality on any mechanical questions.

Sedberry's Drug Store

One of the leading drug stores of Jefferson is Sedberry's. It has been in business in Jefferson since 1865, and is said to be the oldest drug store in Texas, or even in the United States, continuing under the same name. For more than 75 years this store has been serving the people of this and surrounding territory carefully and efficiently.

THE KELLY PLOW WORKS

The name Kelly has been identified with East Texas iron ore development since the Civil War and Reconstruction days. But in order to have a better appreciation of the Kelly family we copy from a paper that was prepared by Hubert M. Harrison, vice president and general manager of East Texas Chamber of Commerce, and a copy was sent to Mrs. McKay, a relative, by Mr. R M. Kelly. It follows.

"About seven years after the historic Battle of San Jacinto, while Texas was a republic, John A. Stewart, later a brother-in-law of G. A. Kelly, came to Texas from Tennessee and began making small crude plows in a little shop operated by a man named Saunders, near Marshall, Harrison County, Texas.

"Five years later, in 1848, Stewart moved his plow patterns and tools to a popular campsite for wagoners called "Four-Mile-Branch," four miles west of the then thriving old Jefferson. Here he formed a partnership with Zachariah Lockett (a brother-in-law) and the new firm of Lockett & Stewart continued making the little plows and operated a general repair shop.

"Jefferson, founded in 1836, was head of navigation in Cypress Bayou, a small tributary of Red River and before the advent of railroads was the metropolis of North Texas and trading center of a vast surrounding area.

"George Addison Kelly, of pioneer Scotch-Irish ancestors came to Texas in 1852. He was born in 1832 in Green County, Tennessee, the seventh of twelve children. At the age of 17 he, with part of the family, migrated to Louisiana and located in a homestead grant in Natchitoches Parish. His pioneer spirit urged him toward Texas and three years later young George, 20 years old, landed in Jefferson via steamboat on which he was a mate Believing this busy frontier held opportunities for an ambitious young man, he located at 'Four Mile Branch' and began his career in the little shop by the side of the road. He soon acquired an interest in this primitive industry and later purchased full ownership.

"The first crude cupola for melting iron in the little foundry used Charcoal and the blast was produced by horse driven bellows. The little shop prospered and expanded and a steam engine and improved cupola were soon installed. Its products were the original crude plow, cast iron stoves ,cooking utensils and machinery repairs. The camping wagons wanted cow bells for their grazing oxen and cattle and the little shop made cow bells—thousands of them.

"Farmers were needing and demanding more and better plows. George A. Kelly met this urgent demand by designing in 1860 the famous 'Kelly Blue Plow', the foundation stone of this near-century-old industry. A tribute at the time of his death in 1909 stated: 'Here is a pioneer who made a plow—and a plow made Texas.'

"From the erstwhile little shop at 'Four-Mile-Branch', renamed Kellyville in honor of its founder, the many camping wagoners, after disposing of their farm and ranch produce in Jefferson, hauled plows and other products throughout the expanding Southwest and the name KELLY became a household word.

"During the Civil War and Reconstruction days iron was very scarce; so this pioneer industrialist built a furnace, and from the abundant East Texas ores smelted high grade pig iron for his own use and sold surplus tonnage, which met with great favor. Charcoal was used for fuel, but this was costly and could not compete with later developed cheaper coke fuels, and after several years of successful operation this furnace was abandoned, having served its useful purpose. This early day iron maker predicted that when the need appeared for iron and steel produced from East Texas ores, an economical fuel process would be developed. Fulfillment of this prediction is near. Large smelters are being constructed at Daingerfield and Houston, Texas, and a gas fired furnace providing sponge iron is near completion in Longview.

"Soon after the outbreak of the Civil War, G. A. Kelly raised a company of soldiers, was commissioned captain and reported for service. His company was accepted but he was detailed to continue producing plows and utensils needed by civilians, also cast iron for cannon balls.

"When railroads began to cross Texas, the wagoners with their long wagon trains gradually disappeared from the rough, muddy roads. Boats ceased to ply the bayou and the important trading center of Jefferson lost its prestige. Then the Kelly foundry and factory were totally destroyed by fire, with no insurance. In 1882 salvage from the wreck was moved to Longview, a new railroad center.

"Beginning anew in Longview, this rebuilt plow factory gradually expanded into an imposing agricultural implement factory—'the lengthened shadow of one man.' Here is manufactured from raw material a wide variety of plows and implements for all types of farms, including the old

'Blue Plow,' which has retained its popularity for almost a century, a continuing tribute to its inventor.

"Operating profits in part were re-invested and the present substantial structure has been built entirely from earnings Full ownership is still in the Kelly family.

"Among the family relics is the 200-pound bell (part silver) used by the boat which brought the ambitious Kelly to Texas, also one of his old cow bells and an antique plow.

"In recognition of this pioneer industry, the Texas Highway Commission erected a granite marker on the original site of the little plow shop at 'Four Mile Branch'.

"This pioneer industry, the only full line plow factory in the Southwest, for nine decades has had only two president-managers, the founder, George A. Kelly, and his son, Robert Marvin Kelly, now president. Since the days of the Republic of Texas, nearly 100 years, from the 'Little shop by the side of the road' and from its present well equipped factory, The G. A. Kelly Plow Company, through prosperity and adversity has continuously supplied plow tools to 5 generations of farmers in Texas and adjoining states. "Truly civilization follows the plow."

SMELTER WAS BUILT IN 1887

About 1887, John A. Crews, of Chicago, promoted a 60-ton furnace to smelt the surface deposits of iron ore found near Orr Switch and Lassater on the L. A. & T. railroad.

The smelter operated intermittently from 1887-1905, under changing managerships, until the high cost of transporting coke for fuel for the furnace made profitable operation impossible.

Several governmental—federal as well as state—investigations and surveys were made of the ore pits in an effort to ascertain the possibility of profitable exploitation.

Had the navigability of the bayou remained unchanged, it is highly possible that Jefferson might have regained the prominence and prosperity it enjoyed during the days of the great river traffic.

The Nash Iron Works

The Nash Iron Works was built in 1847—was operated by Boose and Ab Nash—and was located eighteen miles west of Jefferson on the Coffoeville road.

The main output consisted of wash pots, all kinds of kettles and kitchen utensils, and cannon balls.

In connection with the Iron Works, there was operated a pottery, where plates, bowls, pipes and jugs from 1 quart size to ten gallons, were made.

Those plants were in operation during the war, but no records exist as to how long after the war.

HOMES

Beginning with what is known as the Presbyterian Manse, and was, in the early days, known as the Gen. Rogers home we have what is conceded to be the oldest home in Jefferson, though along with this may be mentioned the following:

The stately mansion of the late W. P. Schluter stands out as a monument to the city. The home has remained in the Schluter family since it was built many, many years ago and is located on Line Street.

The S. W. Moseley home was built by Mr. J. C. Preston, later known as the Norward home. It is said to have been built without nails in the building, only wooden pegs being used and all of the large windows were made by hand.

Another of the old homes is that of Dr. A. A. Terhune, just west of this is the home of Mr. and Mrs. Brennon Whelan, which was built in the early '50's by W. K. Mayberry, brother of Mrs. T. J. Rogers. Just north is another of the early homes, the McKay home. While it was not built by the McKays, they have owned, and it has been occupied by some member of the McKay family for years back. Today it is owned by Mr. and Mrs. Arch McKay. Mrs. DeGraffeuried, daughter of Mr. and Mrs. Norsworth, who spent her childhood in Jefferson came to the old home and asked permission to go all over the place—"peep into the closets" and even to climb the back fence—all of which was gladly permitted by Mrs. McKay. And so happy memories linger in the old home for those who have long since moved to other cities and states. They love to come "home" and all true Jeffersonians are always glad to welcome them.

On Broadway stands a spacious home, that numbers among the oldest and was built by Mr. Alley, father of Mr. Tuck Alley. It is claimed to be about 85 years old. It is built upon a high terrace and to the younger generation has been known as the W. B. Ward, the Sol Spellings, and now the Brewer home. It is a most comfortable colonial home and has just recently been repaired by Miss Florence Weil niece of Mr. Brewer, and the present owner. Miss Weil makes her home in Riverside, California.

The home of Miss Willie Rowell is considered among the early homes of Jefferson and was owned and occupied by Mr. Quincy Bateman and family during the thriving days of Jefferson. The antique furniture in the Rowell home today brings many expressions of appreciation for things so beautiful, and it is considered a privilege to enjoy the treat of being permitted to "take a peep".

The present home of Judge T. D. Rowell was formerly the home of P. G. Graham. After Mr. Graham's death his widow was married to Mr. Overall, who was a printer and had his office and press in the home. The original Graham home was purchased by Judge Rowell and remodeled, being today, a handsome, modern, two story building on Walnut and Henderson Streets.

The J. M. Urquhart home, two miles west of Jefferson, is possibly one of the oldest homes in the immediate territory and has been in the Urquhart family since the early days of Jefferson. It is now the property and home of Mrs. Dessie Urquhart Moseley, granddaughter of Allen Urquhart, who helped in the founding of Jefferson.

Across the highway from this we find another ante-bellum country home, said to have been built by Mr. Ligon, it later became known as the J. C. Preston home and today it is owned by Roy Spellings, where he maintains a dairy. On the place is a scuppernong arbor which produces delicious grapes. The arbor is 60 by 85 feet and one vine measures 16 inches in circumference. The arbor is said to be eighty years old.

The Openheim home, owned and occupied by a member of the family for more than 85 years is among the homes of the early days of Jefferson.

The W. E. Singleton home is one of Jefferson's oldest, and was originally known as the McFarland home. It is now owned and occupied by Mr. and Mrs. Bennie Moseley. Mrs. Moseley is a granddaughter of the late W. E. Singleton Sr.

What is now known as the Jefferson College was originally the B. H. Epperson home and was built in the early '70's. An interesting feature of this building is the stair way and the cupola on the third floor with its specially treated colored glass windows by which water for bathing was heated by the rays of the sun.

DEPARTMENT OF THE INTERIOR
Washington, D. C.
THIS IS TO CERTIFY THAT
THE HISTORIC BUILDING
Known as
William M. Freeman House
IN THE COUNTY OF
Marion
AND THE STATE OF
Texas
HAS BEEN SELECTED BY THE
ADVISORY COMMITTEE OF THE
HISTORIC AMERICAN
BUILDING SURVEY
As Possessing Exceptional
Historic or Architectural
Interest and as Being Worthy
Of Most Careful Preservation
For the Benefit of Future
Generations and That to This
End a Record of its Present
Appearance and Condition
Has Been Made and Deposited
For Permanent Reference in The
LIBRARY OF CONGRESS

Attest:

Marvin Eickeuroht
District Officer

Harold L. Ickes
Secretary of the Interior

The above is a type likeness of a plaque received by Jesse DeWare of Jefferson, used here with his permission. A story of old Jefferson is incomplete without mention of the old Freeman home. This page is explanatory except that it does not have the official seal of the Department of Interior which is on the plaque.

SCHOOLS

Numerous educational institutions had advertisements in the 1871 directory, among them the following:

English and German select school in the Patillo Academy on Benners street—principal, Professor A. Rosentspitz.

St. Mary's School, corner Market and Henderson streets—Teachers, Sisters of Charity.

Collegiate Institute, for male and female, corner Broadway and Alley streets—Principal, Professor J. T S. Parks, Vice Principal, Professor M. Parks.

School for Boys and Girls on Friou street of which Professors P. Calhoun and G. A. Calhoun were principals.

Christ Church School for girls—Rev. E. G. Benners, Rector. Mrs. Kirkpatrick and Mrs. Simmons were teachers.

Other teachers of an early day were Prof. Draper, Mr. Foster, Mr. Jess Benten, Mr. Pickens, a red whiskered Irishman, and Miss Mahala Halloway who taught in the basement of the old Methodist Church.

Mr. Sam Ward organized the Paradise Academy near Jefferson in 1867.

Cal. Bass taught a mixed school in the old courthouse, now the colored school.

Mr. R. W. Vinson and wife taught a private school and later when the public school was established, Mrs. Vinson became one of the charter teachers A few years ago she voluntarily resigned but she is still deeply interested on all educational subjects.

Prof. Looney was one of the early day teachers, as was Miss Maggie Godfrey and Mrs. Willie Owens.

Miss Mary Boise taught a girls school with Mrs. Maggie Preston as assistant.

The Jefferson Institute was another early day school of which Miss Ellie Norwood was principal.

A public school was established in Jefferson in 1888 or '89 with Col. Bass as the first Superintendent.

Mr. R. W. Vinson was the first County Superintendent and Miss Alice Emmert was the second.

PROMINENT CITIZENS OF JEFFERSON IN HER EARLY DAYS

Many of the prominent men who had a part in the making of Texas were born and reared in the little historic town of Jefferson. Mrs. Anna Hardwick Pennybacker was living in Jefferson and wrote the greater part of her "History of Texas" while here. Her father, Dr. J. B. Hardwick, was pastor of the First Baptist Church in Jefferson.

Col. D. B. Culberson

Col. Culberson was congressman from the First Congressional District for twenty-two years. He was one of the leading lawyers of the State, and was prominent in the famous Abe Rothchild case. He was the father of

C. A. Culberson, who was born and reared in Jefferson and started his political career as County Attorney of Marion County and was later Attorney General of the State, Governor of Texas, and was elected to the Senate of the United States. He was known as Senior Senator for a number of years—until his death.

Rev D. B. Culberson, the father of Col. Culberson was one of the early pastors of the First Baptist Church of Jefferson.

W. L. Crawford

A leading criminal lawyer of Texas. Upon leaving Jefferson he moved to Dallas.

Hector McKay

Hector McKay, born in Tennessee, came to Texas with his mother and family when very young, settled near Elysian Fields, where the family remained many years. The old McKay burying ground is there. He was a member of Ector's Brigade during the Civil War, enlisting at Marshall. He attained the rank of Captain. After the war, he practiced law in Marshall where he was a law partner of Judge Mabry and later of W. T. Armstead. Captain McKay was one of the prominent lawyers of early days of Jefferson.

Captain Moss

Captain Moss, the grandfather of Mrs. Will Sims, of Jefferson, in 1836 operated and owned one of the finest steamboats on the river—The Hempstead. He assisted Captain Shreve in blowing out the rafts to make Cypress Bayou navigable to Jefferson and during the Mexican war he transported soldiers across the river into Texas .

Mr. T. L. Lyon

Mr. T. L. Lyon, with his family, came to Jefferson during the summer of 1867. For many years Captain Lyon was a member of the firm, Mooring and Lyon, buying cotton and doing general mercantile business on Dallas Street. They commanded a wide scope of business in the palmy days of the city.

Later in life business reverses came and he accepted a clerkship in the "Lessie 13" a small freight packet, which burned. After which Captain Lyon was clerk on the Alpha. Both boats were commanded by the late Captain Ben Bonham.

Capt. Lyon continued his service on the Alpha, for a number of years. He was a good citizen, a devout Christian and an active member of the Methodist Church until his death Nov 28th, 1908, leaving many friends to mourn his loss.

A daughter, Mrs. G. M Jones, occupied the old home which was bought at the time of her father's coming to Jefferson sixty-nine years ago, until her death recently.

Royal A. Ferris

Mr. Ferris was a leading lawyer of Dallas, Texas, and he too was reared in Jefferson.

Nelson Phillips

Chief Justice of the Supreme Court of Texas, and a leading lawyer of the State, made his home in Dallas and was a product of Marion County, living near Jefferson.

W. B. Harrison

A leading business man and banker of Ft. Worth, Texas for many years started his business career in Jefferson during the palmy days.

The Bateman Family

(King, Andy, and Quincy)

This prominent family in the business and social life of the early days of Jefferson, branched out into the business world in Jefferson and when Jefferson began to lose navigation, along with it, many of her population, the Bateman family moved west and were helpful in building Ft. Worth, Texas, in business and banking lines.

In fact Jefferson furnished many of the leading business and professional men, who went west in the early days and built the State of Texas.

Jefferson is truly the "mother city" of the State of Texas as it was the largest and most noted in the early '70's and gave to the balance of the State leading business and professional men to make "The Lone Star State" great.

The old families, who were not so famous, but were the real stamina of the town down through the ages, when prosperity had passed on to other fields and living was hard—yet they lived on and kept the home fires burning until today Jefferson seems doomed to again come to be, and is known the state over as a promising oil center—with prosperity again in view. These with their children may be numbered by the hundreds. Among them we find:

Dr. B. J. Terry	R. B. Walker
Dr. T. H. Stallcup	W. B. Kennon
W. B. Stallcup	J. B. Zachery
Ward Taylor	W. B. Sims
Dick Terry	D. C. Wise
J. H. Rowell	A. Urquhart
S. W. Moseley	S. A. Spellings
Shep Haywood	Capt. Lyon
T. L. Torrans	A. Stutz
W. P. Schluter	T. J. Rogers
Louis Schluter	W. J. Sedberry

Sam Moseley
W B Ward
Sam Ward
J. M. DeWare
B. J. Benefield

J. C. Preston
P. Eldridge
I Goldberg
M Bower
J J. Rives

H. Rives

These with many others have done much for Jefferson and Texas—
So "Come to Texas" and be sure you come to Jefferson.

Benj. H. Epperson

Benj. H. Epperson was born in Mississippi in about 1828. He was educated in North Carolina and at Princeton University New Jersey. He came to Texas and settled at Clarksville sometime in the '40's. He studied law, was admitted to the bar and practiced with marked ability and success He was active Whig politician before and after the war and was the candidate of his party for governor in 1851 at a time when he was below the constitutional age. In 1852 he was at the head of the Texas delegation to the Whig National convention. He served in the Legislature practically from 1858 until his death He was a personal friend of Sam Houston and was consulted by Houston on numerous affairs of state.

In the controversy over secession Epperson was a Union man, standing substantially with General Houston on that question. After Texas seceded he cast his allegiance with the Confederacy and did a great deal for the cause, giving very liberally of his time and money. He was a member of the first Confederate Congress.

In 1866 he was elected to the U. S. Congress and went to Washington, but as Texas was not recognized as a State, he was not permitted to take his seat.

In the early '70's he moved to Jefferson, Texas where he lived until his death in 1878.

Because of his wide personal acquaintance and unusual ability he exercised a wide political influence throughout the State. He was one of the first presidents of East-Line Railroad, and was highly instrumental in the railroad development of Texas.

In 1931 a collection of papers and letters that had belonged to B. H. Epperson were sent to the University of Texas by his son. Among them were letters dealing with affairs in Texas during the Confederate war and Reconstruction periods, also Indian papers saved from the time that Mr. Epperson had represented the Indians in Washington before, or in the early '50's, besides many papers pertaining to Railway matters, etc. The Archivist, Mrs. Mattie Austin Hatcher has written that "they are very valuable." He says that these things are used by historians and also by students in getting material for their thesis.

[34]

W. P. Torrans

W. P. Torrans, born in Mobile, Alabama, in 1849 moved to Houston, Texas and in 1850 came to Jefferson. He established a general mercantile business on Austin Street, in the building next to the present Goldberg Feed Store.

In 1862 he was Tax Collector, but maintained his business also. In 1872 built the first brick block on Polk Street, where the Torrans Manufacturing Company is now located.

The W. P. Torrans home at one time stood in the middle of this block, made into an office building and used by Dr. A. C. Clopton. Mr. Torrans bought a home on the corner of Lafayette and Market Streets which is standing and in good repair.

The Torrans business has run continuously all these years and is known as the Torrans Manufacturing Company, a very flourishing business, owned and operated by T. L. Torrans, who is one of Jefferson's most prominent and active citizens, and a son of W. P. Torrans, Mr. T. L. Torrans married Miss Elizabeth Schluter, daughter of the late Mr. and Mrs. Louis Schluter, who was a very prominent lawyer in this city.

Tom Lee Torrans, Jr., a son of Mr. Torrans, is now active manager of the store. Mrs. Kelly Spearman and Louis Torrans are also children of Mr. and Mrs. Tom Torrans.

Story From Past Recalls Worth of Two Jefferson Men
Captain DeWare, Col. H. McKay, Have Sons Prominent Here Now

"Before the final adjournment of district court and during a short recess Saturday evening, at Jefferson, the friends of Sheriff J. M. DeWare of Marion County presented him with a Smith and Wesson forty-four caliber pistol and belt. The weapon was elaborately carved, pearl handled, inlaid with gold, and bore this inscription: "J. M. DeWare, Sheriff, Jefferson, Texas. From his friends, Jan. 1, 1887." A graceful and appropriate presentation speech was delivered by Col. McKay.

Taken from the "Dallas and Texas fifty years ago" column in the Dallas News on Jan. 25, the story above was sent The Jefferson Journal by Ollie B. Webb, Texas and Pacific official, with the notation that "it seems to me will be of interest to many in Jefferson."

Mr. Webb was right. As he goes on to explain, Sheriff J. M. DeWare, or Captain DeWare, as he was more generally known, was the father of J. M DeWare, present local agent for the Texas and Pacific in Jefferson, and the Col. H. McKay mentioned, was the father of Arch McKay, now Tax Assessor-Collector.

Both were men who stood out as leaders in their time. Both they and their descendants have many friends in Jefferson.

James Jackson Rives

James Jackson Rives came to Jefferson from Caddo Parish, La., before the Civil War, and established a cotton and hide business after returning from the war. When his son, Herbert Rives, returned from Sewanee Military Institute he joined the business of J. J. Rives and Son, which continued until the warehouse was destroyed by fire about 1902.

R. Ballauf, Merchant and Banker

Rudolph Ballauf was born in Hamburg, Germany, June 30, 1832. At the age of 16 years he sought his fortune in America. Arriving at New Orleans, La., he obtained employment. Later he obtained a position with the Mallory Steamship Lines and gradually worked up to the position as interpreter He was serving in this capacity when the war between the states was declared and he joined the Confederate Army.

He was married in 1866 to Miss Mary Louise Hottinger of New Orleans. To this union seven children were born—Lula (Mrs. D. P. Alvarez), Julia (Mrs. Asa E. Ramsey), Mamie (Mrs. I. L. Goldberg), Corine, George Henry, Emma (Mrs. Eugene Meyer), and Fred W.

Mr. Ballauf came to Jefferson in 1867, he and his wife making the trip by boat.

He opened a general merchandise on the corner of Marshall and Austin streets, later moving to Walnut and Lafayette and later to Austin street. The G. A. Kelly foundry of Kellyville was purchased by Mr. Ballauf and the material used for all manufactured articles was secured in Marion county. Mr. Ballauf operated the foundry until 1895. His mercantile business was later devoted entirely to hardware and mill machinery.

Along with Mr Ballauf's mercantile business a private bank was opened in 1885 and operated as "R. Ballauf and Co." The bank was operated in the office of the store by his three daughters, Lula, Julia and Mamie.

Mr. Ballauf sold his business to his son Fred and his son-in-law Eugene Meyer in 1897, the banking business was discontinued and Mr. Ballauf retired from business having spent thirty years without a failure, assignment or compromise with creditors.

He was an active member of the General Dick Taylor Confederate Camp.

Mr. Ballauf died in 1910. The business established by him has continued through these 69 years and is today successfully operated by his grandchildren under the name of Eugene Meyer and Son.

Robert Potter

March 3, 1843, Senator Robert Potter, a signer of the Texas Declaration of Independence and first secretary of the Navy of the Republic, was murdered at his home on Caddo Lake.

He was born in Gainesville, North Carolina, in 1800. Served in the U. S. Navy from 1815 to 1817, then he returned home and studied law and in 1826 he moved to Halifax and practiced law. He served in the legislature in North Carolina; was elected to the House of Representatives of the 21st United States Congress as a Jackson Democrat. His course was brilliant and improving.

His brilliancy, connected with the fact that he had been a midshipman, led to his appointment in the Cabinet of President Burnett as the first secretary of the Navy of the Republic. He was expelled from the House of Representatives of the Legislature of North Carolina for cheating at cards.

Potter later moved to a place twenty-five miles northeast of Jefferson, Texas, now known as Potter's Point.

A feud arose between Potter and a Captain William Pickney Rose, who was known as the "Lion of the Lakes." The feud arising from the claims that Potter had prevailed upon President Lamar to offer a reward for Rose.

The widow of Rose's brother settled on a league of land claimed by Potter. This was intensified when Rose espoused the candidacy of John B. Denton, who was defeated for a seat in the Senate by Potter.

Potter, who lived on a bluff overlooking Caddo Lake organized a posse of about twenty-five men, surrounded the home of Rose with the intention of capturing, chastising and probably killing Rose.

Rose was near by with some slaves clearing a woodland and when he saw Potter's men, he lay upon the ground while one of his slaves, "Uncle Jerry," piled brush over him and effectually concealed him from view.

Foiled in their purpose, the posse returned and were followed, at a safe distance, by Preston Rose, a son of Captain Rose, who saw them disband; most of them going to Smithland, while nine went with Potter to his home. That night Rose secured "warrant for trespass" against Potter. This was placed in the hands of a Constable, who summoned a posse, consisting of Rose, Preston Rose, J. W. Scott and thirteen others to execute the warrant, as if a warrant for trespass required "the body to be taken." They reached Potter's home at midnight and surrounded it. At daybreak the bodyguard of Potter began to reconnoiter the premises, when Hesekiah George came suddenly upon Captain Rose. Upon being commanded to surrender he turned for flight and gave the alarm. Rose fired both barrels of his shotgun at him and although he survived the wounds he was ever afterwards known as "Old Rose's Lead Mine." Potter became alarmed and ran about a hundred yards to the lake. Being an excellent diver, he plunged into the water and disappeared from sight, but when he came up for air, John W. Scott killed him. He was buried on Potter's Point.

Rogers National Bank

Captain T. J. Rogers, founder of the Rogers National Bank of Jefferson, and one of Jefferson's oldest citizens, was born in 1832, in Hinds

County, Mississippi In 1849 he came to Texas with his father and family In 1856 in Gilmer, Texas, he married Emily Mayberry and they moved to Jefferson, living in what is now known as the Brewer home, with the family of Dr. B. J Terry. During the Civil War, he served in the Confederate Army in General Ochiltree's regiment (the 18th) in General Waul's division, as a lieutenant, later being made captain, after Captain John Cocke, brother-in-law, was killed, in the battle of Mansfield After the war he returned to Jefferson, again engaging in the mercantile business. In 1868 he went into business for himself. He was identified with the material, civic and religious interests of Jefferson. He was one of the promoters of the East Line and Red River railroad (later a branch of the M. K and T. railroad of Texas.) He was secretary and treasurer of this railroad until it was sold to the M. K. and T. He was also principal owner of the Jefferson Cotton Oil Mill, later selling his interests to the Jefferson Cotton Oil Company, which operated until it was burned in 1903.

In 1896 the banking business, T. J. Rogers & Son, was founded in connection with the mercantile business which was now under the name T. J. Rogers & Son, (Ben Rogers).

In 1904 T. J. Rogers & Son, bankers, was nationalized, becoming the Rogers National Bank of Jefferson, with T J Rogers president and B. F. Rogers active vice-president. In 1904 Herbert A. Spellings was elected cashier, which position he held until 1918 when he succeeded to the presidency by reason of the death of Capt. T. J. Rogers, in the meantime B. F. Rogers, vice president, had withdrawn active participation in the bank's management.

Shortly after Mr. Spellings became president the bank became one of the honor banks of the United States and maintained this position to the present time, and throughout the most depressing period the banks have ever faced the Rogers National Bank of Jefferson under Mr. Spellings' guidance maintained more than its legal reserve, willingly met the demands made upon his bank and was never embarrassed to the least extent

When the national moratorium was declared and conservators were being appointed for the safety management of national banks. It was freely stated that the Rogers National Bank had had a conservator for many years in the person of Mr. Spellings, therefore the government would not be called upon to appoint one for that bank, and this bank was one of the first in the United States to re-open without a special examination. Mr. Spellings remained as president until the summer of 1935 when he was removed by death and was succeeded by Mr. Rogers Rainey as president. Mr. Rainey being a grandson of Capt T. J. Rogers, and nephew of Ben F Rogers, the founder of the bank, which is the only bank in Marion County, and an outstanding one in the State of Texas.

ONLY ONE BANK IN FIVE CAN QUALIFY FOR THIS HONOR

What is a "Roll of Honor" bank, and what does it mean to you as

[38]

a depositor, or as a possible depositor, that this institution has been given that rating in the banking "hall of fame?"

A "Roll of Honor" bank is a bank that has voluntarily provided double protection for its depositors by building up its surplus and undivided profits account to a point where this reserve fund is equal to, or greater than the capital of the bank.

The laws, either National or State, do not require any bank to provide this "extra measure of safety." As a matter of fact, the soundest banking practice and the legal requirements of some states fix 20 per cent of the bank's capital as a sufficient reserve fund to maintain for the safety of its depositors.

But before a bank can become known as a "Roll of Honor" bank, it must voluntarily build up its surplus reserve fund to an amount at least five times the usual requirements. So severe are the requirements that only one bank in five in the entire country can qualify as a "Roll of Honor" institution.

The fact that this bank has achieved this distinction stamps it as one of the strongest institutions for its size in the whole United States.

You can see, therefore, that it does mean a great deal to you as a depositor or as a possible depositor, that this is a "Roll of Honor" bank. In addition to giving you "more than the law requires" in protection, we are only striving to give you a "double measure" of courteous and friendly service.

David Browning Culberson

David Browning Culberson was born in Troupe County, Georgia, Sept. 24th, 1830; was educated at Brownwood, La., and Grange, Ga., and studied law under Chief Justice Chilton of Alabama.

He was married to Miss Eugenia Kimball, a lady of sterling character and brilliant mind. It was to her influence and encouragement that he owed a large measure of his success. To this union three children were born, Charles A., the oldest, was one year old when the family moved to Texas in 1856. Robert Owen and a daughter, Anna, were born in Texas. Robert Owen is the only surviving one. He now resides in Houston, Texas.

The Culberson family—Jim Culberson, a brother with his family and Dr. R. L. Rowell and family, and others and a large company of slaves came to Texas in covered wagons.

Dr. Rowell located in Jefferson but the Culberson brothers moved to Gilmer, Texas, where they practiced law for two years, then came to Jefferson to make their home.

Col. D. B. Culberson was elected to the State Legislature in 1859, was elected again in 1864. He was then elected to the Forty-fourth Congress and served continuously until his death.

From a private in the Confederate Army he was promoted to the rank of Colonel of the 18th Texas Infantry, was assigned to duty in 1864 as Adjutant-General, with rank of Colonel.

Although a nationally known lawyer of shrewd and brilliant mind he remained always unassuming almost careless in his dress. In manner he was shy and retiring.

He spoke so seldom in Congress that he was known as "The Silent Member."

His brilliant mind, sterling qualities of character won for him the title of "Honest Dave." He was one of the lawyers in the famous Diamond Bessie-Rothchild case.

The Rev. D. B. Culberson, Sr., the father of Col. Culberson was one of the early pastors of the First Baptist Church of Jefferson.

CLUBS

The 1881 Club

The 1881 Club was organized in Jefferson, Texas in October 1881 at the home of Mrs. W. B. Ward, where a room full of enthusiastic members organized a chautauqua circle. Among the charter members were: Mrs. J. H. Bemis, Mrs. J. P. Russell, Mrs. Sallie Dickson and Miss Sarah Terhune. The circle was composed of both men and women and met at night. Captain J. P. Russell was the first president with Ben Epperson as Secretary. At the end of four years diplomas and credits were given.

Without a break in the meetings the chautauqua circle was merged into a woman's club, called the Review Club lessons being taken from current magazines, then known as the Shakespearean Club for several years.

Finally in 1882 when it became a member of the State and Third District Federation the name was changed to "The 1881 Club" in honor of the year of its organization. Many have been the courses of study by the enthusiastic members. In fifty-five years of its existence the club meetings have continued each week, only disbanding from second Saturday in May to the first Saturday in October. One of the charter members, Mrs. Sarah Terhune Taylor, is now an honorary member. One of the active members, Mrs. D. C. Wise dates her membership to 1896. This club has the distinction of being the oldest club in the State of Texas.

THE WEDNESDAY MUSIC CLUB

The Wednesday Music Club is one of the oldest music clubs in the state, having been organized in 1909 by the late Mrs. W. H. Mason, for the purpose of study and to assist the 1881 Club in putting on a program when the 1881 Club entertained the Third District Federation of Women's Clubs in 1910.

[40]

The Music Club requested membership in the Federation at this meeting and was a member of the Federation of Woman's Clubs until the Music Club began a separate organization.

The members of the club who are now living are:

Mrs. Addie Terry Nance, Lebannon, Oregon.
Mrs. G. T. Haggard, Jefferson, Texas.
Mrs. J. M. DeWare, Jefferson, Texas.
Mrs. Mattie Vines, Jefferson, Texas.
Mrs. S. S. Minor, Jefferson, Texas.
Miss May Belle Hale, Jefferson, Texas.
Miss Eva Eberstadt, Jefferson, Texas.
Mrs. Murph Smith DeWare, Jefferson, Texas.
Mrs. J. A. Nance was the first president of the club.
Mrs. Mattie Vines, first director.
Miss Ethel Leaf (Mrs. J. M. DeWare) first accompanist.

The first choruses "Carmen" and "In Old Madrid" were presented at the District meeting of Federated Women's Clubs.

The Wednesday Music Club was a member of the East Texas Music Festival during its seven years of existence and with the May Belle Hale Symphony Orchestra, as Co-Hostess, entertained the Festival in May 1924.

Mrs. H. A. Spellings was president of the East Texas Festival at this time also president of The Wednesday Music Club, serving the club in this capacity for fourteen years.

Mrs. G. T. Haggard was the Club president last year and she and Mrs. Furrh Smith DeWare are the only members who have served the club, uninterruptedly from its beginning.

The Club had the honor and pleasure of taking part in the wedding of one of its members, Miss Ethel Leaf to Mr. J. M. DeWare by rendering "Lohengrin's Wedding March." This really was a "few" years back but a happy memory to those present on such a joyous occasion.

MARION COUNTY

Possibly few counties have the distinction of having been a part of so many other counties as has Marion County, so no wonder she is so "tiny" in size after having been sliced and served to six different others.

The records at Austin, Texas, tell us that Marion County was first a part of Red River County, later a part of Shelby, Bowie, Titus, Cass and Harrison. Cass County was for ten years known as Davis County. Thus again taking the name of Cass, so really another "slice" may have been taken off Marion.

However it is up to Harrison for being the "big hearted" county. Years ago a negro representative was sent to the Legislature from Harrison County and during his term of office Marion County acquired a nice acreage of Harrison County, and when the Negro Representative returned to Marshall he was asked "Why in the mischief did you allow anything like that to happen?", he replied: 'Well Sir, Senator Culberson just talked me right out of that little piece of land.' "

Marion County today has an abundant supply of high grade iron ore; saw mills, chair factory, an abundant supply of the purest and best artesian water to be found any where. The county is well adapted to the raising of hogs and cattle. The most delicious sweet potatoes, fruit and berries of all kinds Mayhaws grow wild and from these is made a most palatable and beautiful jelly; in fact almost anything will do well in Marion County. There are many kinds of clover growing wild.

STERN MEMORIAL FOUNTAIN

Stern Memorial Fountain was given to the City of Jefferson by the children (Eva, Leopold, Alfred and Fred) of Jacob and Ernestine Stern in 1913.

In the gift of this splendid piece of work lay the life time love of Jefferson, a devotion of a little immigrant girl grown to womanhood, and the gratitude of her children to a little city that had given Mother and Father happiness.

The fountain is entirely of purest bronze and is 13½ feet high, with bowls of 7½ feet broad, and has a statue six feet tall representing "L'ducation,' the total cost being $4,000.

Engraved on the fountain is· "Dedicated in honor of Jacob & Ernestine Stern, who lived in Jefferson for many years. Presented to the City of Jefferson by their children as an expression of affection for their native town".

More than seventy-six years ago, Mr. and Mrs. Stern came to Jefferson from Houston, in a two horse wagon. Mr. Stern was buried in Jefferson in 1872 and later the family went to New York to live.

The fountain is still used, as was originally intended, for the good of man, stock and dogs, and the pure water that flows through it was given the ladies of Jefferson by the late W. B. Ward in appreciation for work done in the prohibition election many years ago.

As the people of Jefferson appreciated the noble qualities of the Stern family, they too appreciate the gift of love from the children.

In connection with the foregoing article a little book has been written by Mr. Stern's sister-in-law, Mrs. Eva Stern, a most beautiful token of the noble lives of Mr. and Mrs Stern.

In the book is printed a bill-of-sale for a negro woman slave. When Mr. Stern gave the bill-of-sale to his wife he said, "I felt like a mean creature when I paid the money for that girl, but I knew that we needed a nurse girl . . . so what was to be done . . . Where I was born, on the

Rhine, no one would believe for a moment that I would buy a human being. They would hate me, as I hate myself, for bartering in human flesh.

The exact bill of sales for Sarah read as follows:

"Received from Jacob Stern two thousand dollars for a negro woman, by name Sarah, about thirty-four years of age, copper colored. Said woman I promise to deliver to Jacob Stern, in course of six days. I hereby guarantee the woman, Sarah, to be sound in body and mind. I also guarantee said woman, Sarah, to be a good house woman. If not, I promise to take her back and refund to said Jacob Stern $1000."

Just before Mr. Stern's death their old servant "Aunt Caroline" and he were talking and he told her that he thanked God he had set the colored people free, and she replied, "But thanks be to him mos'en fer giben me my good marsar and misses, who gib me my close, my vittles and my medicine."

WALNUT GROVE

Five miles south of Linden there stands today an immense walnut grove. Planted on both sides of the old dirt road, one hundred or more of these trees are all that are left of the 320 planted by Mr. Jim Lockett, more than 60 years ago. The trees make a dense shade and a beautiful lane.

The story is, that Mr. Lockett in a reminiscent mood, thought, that the country some day would run out of split rails, with which to make fences. Realizing that wire would some day be used for making fences he knew that fence posts would be needed, so he ordered his farm hands to plant in every other corner of the rail fence a slim seedling walnut tree to be used for future fence posts.

They are standing today waiting for the wife and we are told that when the new highway was built that it was moved over 200 feet to keep from injuring the roots of Mr. Lockett's trees.

Mr. Lockett passed away more than 20 years ago, but his Walnut line is still a joy to the many who pass that way and many people gather the Walnuts by the bushel each fall.

Another interesting thing that Mr. Lockett had on his farm was his water gin One of the neighbors said, "that in its day it could really go after the cotton."

The water was brought to the gin through a series of ditches and water troughs a mile and a quarter long.

From overhead and controlled by a gate, the water fell onto the top of a large wooden wheel 36 feet in diameter. Around the wheel were attached buckets holding 15 gallons of water each, and when enough buckets were filled with water the wheel began turning and the gin ran. "She would launch out five bales a day, if you got going by daylight."

MURDER ALLEY

"Murder Alley" may be reached by taking the left where Line Street divides, going south to the river, leaving the Barbee home on the right.

The name "Murder Alley" was derived from the fact that one and often two dead bodies would be found each morning in this alley.

Col. Lowery is said to have edited a paper in the Barbee home during these much trying days.

It may be of interest to many Jeffersonians to know that the original courthouse was, according to the Allen Urquhart plan, located just in front of the P. G. Henderson home.

---o---

THE STORY OF DIAMOND BESSIE

This sketch of a famous murder case in Jefferson is mostly from the pen of W. H. Ward who lived at that time and later moved to Texarkana where he was editor of "The Twentieth Century" and this sketch is taken from the December issue, along with a few other legends from other sources.

"The recent mysterious murder of a woman in Jefferson, Texas, recalls the death of Bessie Moore or "Diamond Bessie," who was believed to have been slain by her husband and erstwhile paramour, Abe Rothchild, within rifle shot of where the murder was committed more than twenty years ago.

The murder of Bessie Moore, properly Bessie Rothchild, a young and beautiful woman who had won the sobriquet of Diamond Bessie by the number and splendor of her jewels, was one of the most startling and sensational crimes in the criminal history of Texas. The scene of the crime was visited by thousands of curious spectators and the entire press of the Southwest teemed with gruesome incidents of the awful crime. Crowds came from afar to view the spot where the young mother had been hurled into eternity without warning, carrying with her the half formed life of an unborn infant.

On the shiny slope of a Southern hillside, almost within call of the then thriving populous city of Jefferson, Texas, in the calm of a Sabbath afternoon, the cruel and cowardly crime was committed, for which the husband was twice sentenced to hang but escaped justice by a technicality of the law. The murder of Bessie Rothchild, by the man who was first her betrayer and then her husband, was a crime so weird and terrible that the hand of a master might make it immortal, without for one instant diverging from the strict line of truth into the realm of romance.

Twenty-four years ago, Bessie Moore, the daughter of respectable parents of moderate circumstances, was decoyed from her home in the country by the son of a wealthy Cincinnati family. With the inexperience of youth, and that blind faith which makes a woman follow the man

[44]

she loves to the utmost ends of the earth, Bessie Moore followed Abe Rothchild to Cincinnati. There for one year the young girl was plunged into that maelstrom of sin which whirls and eddies about a great city. Her companions were those of the half-world, the submerged half. Rothchild was rich and he showered his wealth upon the girl from whom he had taken all that life holds dear, home, family and friends.

The motley population of Jefferson added color to the restless movement of the town. The streets were crowded with men of many kinds of dress, cowboys in chaps and spurs, gentlemen in morning coats with canes, farmers in dingy overalls, ladies in elaborate flowing gowns, old slavery negroes, self confident, northern negroes, carpet-baggers, and into the crowd came Bessie Moore, sparkling with diamonds, accompanied by dark and tall Abe Rothchild and did she create a sensation? She was part of this restless life the three short days that she was among them, diamonds sparkled in her ears as she shook her head and laughed, diamonds so large on her fingers that it seemed they must tire her small hands. This poor return for her sacrifice satisfied the girl only for a time, then the glittering jewels, silken raiment, which gave her the sobriquet of "Diamond Bessie" and which were purchased with a woman's shame, began to pall upon her. Bessie Moore was to become a mother.

Amid all the dissipation into which her betrayer had thrust her, the woman had remained true and steadfast to the man she loved, for whom she had given up her innocence and home. Through all this time she had relied upon Rothchild's promise to make her his wife and she prayed that the promise might be fulfilled.

Finding her prayers of no avail she demanded a fulfillment of the pledge. There was a scene, of course, and other scenes followed but Rothchild had now to deal, not with a silly trusting girl, but with a wronged, outraged and desperate woman, who battled not only for her rights but for her child, yet unborn. In a fit of desperation she threatened to lay the shameful story of her betrayal before Rothchild's father, a wealthy and influential citizen of Cincinnati. Then Rothchild is alleged to have conceived and proceeded to carry out a crime so dark, so despicable and so diabolical that Satan himself must have blushed at its conception. He promised the young girl to make her his wife, told her that it would not do for them to be married in Cincinnati; where both themselves and their intimacy were so well known, but that he would take her on his western trips. Rothchild was a traveling salesman representing a jewelry house in which his father was financially interested and he himself being slated for partnership, and that they would be married in some out of the way place out west and that by changing one figure in the marriage certificate, it would make it appear that they had been married immediately upon the young girl. leaving home, which would have given legitimate birth to the child, to which Bessie Moore was about to become a mother.

[45]

The girl believed him and bles _d him and they left Cincinnati, together, traveling westward and passing through Texarkana. From the moment Rothchild promised to make Bessie Moore his wife he had been planning the woman's murder. They left the Texas and Pacific railway at Kildare, Rothchild telling the woman that they would go through Linden, the County seat of Cass County, to be married, choosing that spot, he said, because it was so obscure that news of the marriage would not be heard outside the little town in which the ceremony was to be performed. His real intention was to murder the woman on the road. He was thwarted in this by being compelled to make the trip on a public coach, there being no such thing as private conveyances in Kildare

Once at Linden, Rothchild was compelled to make good his promise and Bessie Moore, the wronged and betrayed girl became Bessie Rothchild, the wife of her betrayer. From Linden they came to Jefferson, Texas from which point it was agreed that Mrs. Rothchild should return to Cincinnati and have her marriage certificate recorded changing the date, as agreed upon, after which she was to return to her husband. The poor girl looked forward with eagerness and hunger to the day she would return to her home bearing the honored name of wife and be clasped once more in her mother's arms. Alas! The poor girl lies in an obscure corner of the Jefferson Cemetery, her body long since dust and food for worms. They reached Jefferson and registered at the Brooks Home— (now the Foster home.)

From some cause she appeared unhappy and one of the maids of the hotel, who entered the room several times during the afternoon, declared she found Bessie weeping bitterly, but the next morning she seemed to have recovered her cheerfulness and gave the maid a handsome present, telling her that she and her husband had not been very happy for some time past but that they were entirely reconciled and were going out in the woods to spend the day. Lunch was prepared for them at the hotel. They were seen by twenty people to cross the public bridge over Cypress Bayou, within a hundred yards of the business portion of the city. The writer himself, returning from a ride, met them within a hundred yards of the bridge and noticed them only sufficiently to note that they were strangers, fashionably dressed and that the woman was very beautiful.

The couple strolled leisurely along for half a mile on the other side of the bridge, then taking a by path plunged into the forest, climbed a hill, almost within stone's throw of the public thoroughfare, and within rifle shot of the city itself. They had their lunch and doubtless the man who planned one of the most cowardly murders ever perpetrated whispered words of love and loyalty into the ears of the poor woman, only too glad to receive them. Their lunch was spread on a large rock; it was almost an ideal spot, deep in the heart of the woodland, surrounded by the songs of birds and the musical ripple of the running water In the shade of the giant oak and ironwood they whiled away the midday hours. Seated on the moss grown rock, the woman cut the initials of her husband in the soft bark of a curly maple and with a fond woman's foolish heart treasured the false vows of her brutal lord in whose inhuman breast lurked a purpose so dark, so deadly that the fiends of hell must have shuddered at its import. While the foolish heart of the woman fluttered with hope and thrilled with fond desires, the hand of the master murderer of modern times, pushed the rim of a deadly revolver within an inch of her white temple, where rippling masses of sunny hair fell in clustering curls, and without a tremor sent a bullet crashing through her brain. The sound of a shot rang out on the evening air, reverberated from the hillside and died away in distant woods. The birds stopped midway their gladsome song, a tiny serpent of smoke rose above the tree tops and drifted with the winds, a frightened squirrel darted into its den, the sluggish river flowed smoothly at the base of the hill, and a dead white face stared at the winter sky.

With fiendish deliberation the uxorcide removed the costly jewels from the dead form, with one hand the murderer of Bessie Rothchild hurled a hopeless woman's soul into eternity and with the other stripped her lifeless body of the poor gaudy ornaments, which were badges of her shame, the price of a woman's sin.

Rothchild returned to the city by a different route, employing a negro boatman to put him over the river. On his return to the hotel he explained that he left his wife with friends in the country. He left Jefferson the next day and it was not until a week or more that the body was discovered, within a hundred yards of what is known as the Shreveport road, a public highway traveled by hundreds of people daily. The corpse lay for all this time untouched by animals of the forest and unclean birds of the air.

Rothchild was traced to Cincinnati and only a few days intervened before the Sheriff of Jefferson, Mr. John Vines, located him in a saloon and brought him back to Texas. Finding himself surrounded by detectives, fearing every bush an officer, cowering 'neath the lash of an accusing conscience the murderer of Bessie Moore, with the same pistol, which had sent his helpless, hapless victim to her last account, attempted to end his own miserable existence.

Again the pistol was pointed at the temple of human life, but the hand of a suicide was not as steady as that of a murderer, Rothchild lost an eye while Bessie lost her life.

For seven years Abe Rothchild battled for his life with the help of the South's best legal talent against the State's attorneys who accused him of killing Bessie Moore.

After one of the most sensational murder trials in the history of Texas, after being twice convicted and sentenced to hang Rothchild escaped justice through a technicality of the law.

The story goes that when the verdict of the jury was given, the foreman of the jury drew a crude picture of a noose on the wall of the courthouse and said: "This is my verdict." The lawyers who defended Abe Rothchild were Mabry, Pierce, McKay, and Culberson, Culberson and Armistad, Crawford and Crawford, Turner and Lipscomb and it is also said that their fees were princely.

W. T. Armistad of the firm of Culberson and Armistad cleared Rothchild.

People came from miles—resentment was strong and for days the battle raged—strangers recognized Rothchild as the same handsome stranger who had spent two days at the Capitol Hotel in Marshall, under the name of Abe Rothchild.

The courthouse where Abe Rothchild was twice tried for the murder of beautiful Bessie Moore, is now used for the negro school and the jail in which he attempted to take his life has long since been torn away.

Rothchild later served a twenty year sentence in a Southern penitentiary for a gigantic system of theft and forgery directed against the Pacific Express Company, with a sufficient number of charges pending against him, in other states to send him to his grave in stripes, though he lived three times the time alloted to man.

This ends the story and history of "Diamond Bessie" which startled the world a score of years ago, with details of which many people in this community are familiar.

Only a small stone marked the humble looking grave and it is told by the sexton that it was donated by a marble yard that formerly did business here. Her name was written in indelible ink and long since has faded away. After she had been buried many years a stranger came into the cemetery and asked to be shown her grave. His visit was an occasion of heart-breaking sobs and bitter tears. He left as he came in an unbroken silence as to who he was, or from whence he came.

The body of this beautiful girl was placed in a casket that was bought by the big hearted citizenship of Jefferson costing $150.

Just beyond the wagon bridge, on the road leading to Marshall and Shreveport her heart was pierced by a cruel bullet, from a hand she loved. His only defense was an "alibi" a change of venue was tried, finally in Jefferson and at the verdict "not guilty" the most awful frown of displeasure was seen on the face of the Judge. The name of this girl was Bessie Moore.

THREE "CITIZENS" OF JEFFERSON

"Aunt Viney"

There were three Citizens of Jefferson who were not so prominent but they were well known and will be remembered by the "Children" of forty and fifty years ago.

First we would remind you of "Aunt Viney." Surely there was never another just like her. She was a real African, large of stature, black, kinky headed and had a style all her own. She modeled her robes of "tow sacks," often making them many layers thick, according to the weather. Sometimes her robes were long and again they reached the shins. She "earned" her living by begging from house to house and when the weather was extremely cold she often sought shelter for the night, on the back·porches that were not securely locked. She was never in a hurry to leave and was often aroused by the owner stumbling over her when he came out. She was never known to steal and rarely displayed her temper. She had little to say to anyone but she wielded her long heavy walking stick in a professional manner when the children tormented her and they were not long in retreating.

"Aunt Maria"

Another well known character was "Aunt Maria." She was entirely different from Aunt Viney in appearance and manner. She was tall and slender and wore her dresses trailing in the dust. She would stand for hours, on the street shaking her skirts and speaking fluently to an imaginary audience. She was perfectly harmless unless tormented by the boys who thought it rare fun to tease her.

"Sugar Boy"

Sugar Boy was the son of an adopted daughter of Dr. and Mrs. Walker, a highly respected couple who lived in Jefferson more than fifty years ago.

Barry Benefield, the son of our own Mr. and Mrs. B. J. Benefield, who is a writer of great note has mentioned "Sugar Boy" in his books but he did not tell you that the real "Sugar Boy' was red-headed, freckled and always dirty. He had a better mind than many gave him credit for having. He was always ready to play, but when he grew tired he made it hard for the smaller children while the older boys sent him home in a trot and weeping.

He thoroughly enjoyed snooping around at night to peep in and see what was going on in the neighborhood and to play "tick-tack." He passed away many years ago leaving only one sister who is living in California.

Even though he had a home, he liked to take his plate and push it between the palings to the children in the neighborhood to be served a lunch. Everyone was most generous and kind to him.

JIMPLECUTE

Sixty years of service, with one idea: to upbuild Jefferson and Marion County.

The Jefferson Jimplecute was first issued as a weekly, then semiweekly, daily, then again as a weekly. It never lost an opportunity to advocate every proposed plan that had in it anything that would put Jefferson or Marion County to the front.

The Jefferson Daily Jimplecute founded in 1865 by Col. Ward Taylor, is the only one of twenty-three newspapers, published at one time or another in Jefferson, to endure until the present.

Did you ever stop to think that the name Jimplecute carries with it more meaning than any other name now in use?

Ignorance of this fact has made many think that it meant nothing and was therefore without significance. This demonstrates the fact that nothing should be cast aside without a thorough investigation and we are publishing here, in its entirety, an article written by the late Judge W. T. Atkins of Jefferson, giving to you the various important words that mean much, that go to make up the one word JIMPLECUTE.

WHAT IS THERE IN A NAME

(The following is the last explanation of the word Jimplecute and it is reproduced for this issue.)

Since the compilation of the word JIMPLECUTE, the curious, the thoughtless, and thoughtful, the learned and the unlearned have been curious to know the significance of the word. The linguists of renown have failed to find any trace of the word in any of the live or dead languages. We have at last decided to place before our readers the origin of the word, and let those who have characterized the name as being meaningless see how far wrong they were. We doubt if there is a name carried in the entire newspaper fraternity that has more significance than the JIMPLECUTE. It is the friend of all the elements that builds up the country, it is absolutely free from politics. It is a friend of labor, likewise capital. It advocates industry, and greatest of all it advocates friendship and unity between every interest. When properly written out the JIMPLE-CUTE reads as follows:

Join
Industry
Manufacturing,
Planting
Labor
Energy
Capital, (in)
Unity
Together
Everlastingly

JIMPLECUTE HAS SEEN 23 FAIL

We leave with pride and satisfaction the explanation of the word which has so long been slandered as being meaningless, unpronounceable, and such complimentary econiums. To all such the JIMPLECUTE sends greetings, and in the kindest of spirits says "that he who laughs last, laughs best." While perhaps "a rose would smell as sweet by any other name," yet there is no name that we are familiar with that carries with it so much promise, so much significance, such hope, as that grandest of words, The JIMPLECUTE.

The JIMPLECUTE was established in 1865 by Ward Taylor, Jr., who died in 1894 and his son, and daughter, M. I. Taylor, (known to her many friends as "Miss Birdie") conducted the paper jointly until 1915, when Miss Taylor took entire control and conducted the paper until it was sold in 1926. Miss Taylor retained the job printing department, which she continues managing, and doing the entire work herself these ten years since.

"Miss Birdie" is loved by her friends, and many strangers, passing this way, drop in to see her. She is ever ready to lend a helping hand to anyone in need and to any project for the betterment of her home town. She recalls many of Jefferson's earlier days when it was a real city and by her much of the past history of our little city has been preserved. She recalls the big fire of 1866 even though she was quite young, she says that she and her family were living at the Irvine Hotel (now the Excelsior) and had their clothes and articles that they especially desired to save tied in bundles, so that they might escape in case the hotel burned.

CADDO LAKE

The same shaking up of the earth that made Reel Foot lake in Tennessee caused the sinking of the ground and formation of Caddo Lake with its connecting chain of lakes and Cypress Bayou in Marion County. A dam of logs, the accumulation of years, piled up in Red River, backing the water up into the lake and bayou so as to make them navigable by the largest steam boats.

The fine sandy land adjacent to these lakes produced excellent crops of cotton of the finest grade, and the planters of the Old South had long before the war thrown it into a series of plantations of 5000 acres or more.

Caddo Lake is said to be the most mysterious body of water in Texas. Tourists and campers always find something delightfully unique about the lake. The lake proper is 20 miles long and 16 miles wide. More than 400 oil derricks dot the surface of the lake with a network of pipelines underlying its surface. Mechanics and other employees go from well to well by motor boat.

The greater part of Caddo Lake lies in Marion County Texas with the remainder being in Harrison County, and Caddo Parish, La.

[51]

When the first white settlers came to this locality the Indians told them that the lake was formed overnight in 1812 by some kind of volcanic eruption. Many Indians were said to have lost their lives in the upheaval. The lake is fed by the waters of Cypress Bayou and in former times most of Eastern Texas transportation was carried on by way of the Mississippi, Red, and Cypress rivers and Caddo Lake.

The Federal Government has made several cuts, or ditches as they are known for the purpose of straightening the channel and in these cuts are found many fish as well as some alligators. Catfish weighing more than fifty pounds have been taken from this stream.

Many club houses have been built along the shores of the lake and its tributaries, among them the Dallas, the Caddo, Port Caddo, Greenville, Jefferson-Atlanta, Meyers, Terry, and many others, both private and commercial.

OAKWOOD CEMETERY

It has been truly written that the history of Jefferson—its struggles its earlier fight, its romance—is written in this old cemetery.

From the two iron posts that stand a few feet apart, once joined by iron chains, which marks the resting place of two artists who killed each other and are buried together, chained together, and unnamed, to the tomb erected by the State of Texas over one of Jefferson's leading citizens, and down to the tiny sunken, graves of innumerable infants who died in the middle of the last century, Jefferson's age-old saga is told among the tombs of its ancestors.

General Ochiltree's Tomb

The State of Texas has placed over this famous son a lovely red granite marker, and from this marker we learn that General Ochiltree was Judge of the Fifth District in 1842, Secretary of the Treasury in 1844, and Attorney General of the Republic of Texas in 1845; also that the County of Ochiltree was named for him.

Another monument that passersby regard with reverence is that of D. B. Culberson, long a Senator from this District and father of the Texas Governor, Chas. A. Culberson. The inscription on this monument is simple: "David B. Culberson, Sept. 29, 1830—May 7, 1900—Erected by his sons."

OTHERS. Nancy Ann Waskom, Dated 1819-1852.

Lucy Eason, 1853
Talbot P. Amos, 1852.
Sarah N. Owens, 1857.

Ross Hammett Spellings, father of S. A. Spellings, was buried in 1871.

While an overground iron vault is unique in the story of burials, it houses the body of a two-year-old baby, George Hoffman, and is dated 1870.

"DIAMOND BESSIE"

Almost everyone in the state has heard the story of "Diamond Bessie" and her murder, but not every one knows that a few years ago the Cemetery Committee, Mrs. Arch McKay and Mrs. H. A. Spellings, working late on the grounds, returned early the next morning with their crew of men and found erected on the grave of "Diamond Bessie" a new monument with the simple inscription, "Bessie Moore—12-13-1876." The monument that had marked the grave was entirely removed. The marking of this old monument, having been done in indelible ink, had faded away.

The first stone is said to have been placed over the grave by noble-hearted citizens of Jefferson, but no one, other than the person who placed it on the grave, knows just when the last stone was erected or by whom, though various reports have been circulated—all different. We only know that it was placed between the setting and rising of the sun.

Humor There

There is humor too in the old cemetery. Placed prominently in the center of the headstone, under glass, where it has remained since 1855, is a photograph of a much bearded man. It is a photograph of W. W. Sloan, who was born in 1830 and buried in 1885, and his stern face still rebukes those inclined to take lightly the facts of death and the grave. Mr. Sloan was a photographer in Jefferson for many years.

On another stone there is this rhyme:
"Remember, friend, as you pass by,
As you are now, so once was I,
As I am now, so you must be,
Prepare for death and eternity."

The story is told that once, in charcoal, a wag wrote underneath this inscription:

"Be still, my friend, and rest content,
Until I find out just where you went."

Over on one side of Oakwood Cemetery is the Jewish Cemetery. This plot of ground is said to have been purchased by Mr. Jacob Stern and another citizen, who presented it to the Jewish people of Jefferson for a burying ground. Many Jews have been brought back to the old home town, that their bodies may rest beside loved ones who have gone before.

This cemetery is kept as nicely as these "Chosen people" keep their homes. A low stone wall separates it from Oakwood Cemetery.

[53]

Then on the extreme south side of the Oakwood Cemetery is the Catholic Cemetery, this too, is well kept.

In Oakwood proper which burying ground dates from the time of Reconstruction, many bodies were removed from the Cemetery, in what is today known as "Sandtown." Following the Civil War many Federal soldiers were buried there. This is one mass of shrubs, graves and trees, with few markers, and only a guess can tell one where the soldiers in blue, who died in this part of the world, found their resting place.

One street in the cemetery is known as "The Street of Graves," and the legend goes that many unmarked graves are underneath the street. Should you let your imagination play, you can outline for yourself the dents in the earth that mean graves, as you drive down the street between the rows of modern lots.

Frank Schweers and his father, sextons for the Cemetery for two generations, have buried 9,000 citizens of Jefferson since 1870, when the older Schweers took charge. There are about 14,000 graves in the Cemetery, the oldest having for its inscription: "Rev. Benjamin Foscue—1798-1850" and which is still in a state of good preservation

And so, through almost one hundred years, the history of old Jefferson and new Jefferson is written on the stones in the Cemetery, a valuable, beautiful, romantic history that we should keep intact—that we should value and preserve. ARE YOU DOING YOUR PART?

Rose and Robertson

When "old timers" are in a reminiscent mood you can hear many interesting incidents of the early days of Jefferson, and one that few remember, and often wonder about, is the story of two men whose graves are in Oakwood Cemetery, unmarked other than by two iron posts that were chained together.

Mr. J. E. Hasty knew the men and gives this information: Rose and Robertson let their hatred of each other and their love for a woman, cause them to take the life of each other, a most unusual coincidence.

Rose owned and operated a blacksmith shop on Polk Street near where the Jay Fort home stands. As he was working one day, Robertson, a gambler, came across the street and entered the shop. When Rose saw him coming he turned and started out the rear door, but Robertson had gone there with the determination to kill Rose, so without warning he fired the bullet that killed Rose, who as he went down aimed well and sent a bullet into the heart of his enemy. Robertson walked across the street and sat down upon the sidewalk saying, "that ————— rascal has killed me," and he too passed away.

As a fitting finish they were buried side by side, chained together and only iron posts to mark their resting place.

A few Epitaphs found on some of the stones in Oakwood Cemetery:

"Old Pop"

"Daddy Come Here,   I am Coming"

"Sweet Babe, now quiet"

"God loveth a cheerful giver"

"She hath done what she could"

"I have three little angels waiting
for me on the beautiful banks of the crystal sea.
Not impatiently wait my darlings there, for smiles light up
their brows so fair and their little harps ring out so clear, so
soothingly sweet to faithless listing ears. They live in the smile
of the Savior's love, who so early called my darlings above."

"Weep not for me Carrie dear, I am not dead,
but sleeping here. I was not yours, but Christ's
alone. He loved me best and took me home"

"Just in the morning of this day he died,
In the midst of life we are in death."

"To know her was to love her."

"She has crossed the rocks to rest in the shade."

"On earth she was a dutiful daughter, a loving wife, an
earnest Christian, in Heaven an angel"

"Papa's little girl no longer suffers."

"Gone but not lost"

"Budded on Earth, Blooming in Heaven"

"A loved one has crossed"

"We will not say farewell"

"An honest man is the noblest work of God"

"It is good to have lived, to have loved to have thought."

"As a wife, devoted. As a friend, ever kind and true, in life
she exhibited all the graces of a Christian.'

"Earth has no sorrow that Heaven cannot heal."

"There is a world above where parting is unknown, Formed for
the good alone."

"Gone from our home but not from our hearts"

"It is enough, Come up higher"

"No pains, no griefs, no anxious fear can reach our loved one
sleeping here."

This little story will not be complete without mention being made
of some of the "Belles" of the early days of Jefferson, who are here today
to tell Jefferson's history.

It is a rare treat to have as our guests, Mrs. Ida Rogers Rainey, Mrs.

[55]

Jessie Allen Wise, Mrs. Murph Smith Deware, Mrs. Jennie Lyon Jones and Mrs. Sue Jackson Hale.

It has been the privilege of the writers of this pamphlet to enjoy several "Get-Together Luncheons," and to hear the "girls" tell of their beaux, and the early history of Jefferson, along with the good times they had at school.